MANAGING EDUCATION FOR EFFECTIVE SCHOOLING:

THE MOST IMPORTANT PROBLEM IS TO COME TO TERMS WITH VALUES

John Raven

Trillium Press

Unionville, New York
Toronto, Ontario

Oxford Psychologists Press

311 Banbury Road
Oxford OX2 7JH
England

John Raven
30 Great King St.
Edinburgh EH3 6QH
Scotland

Trillium Services, Inc.

First Avenue

Unionville, NY 10988

(914) 726-4444

FAX: (914) 726-3824

ISBN: 0-89824-531-1

Trillium Services, Inc.

78 Biddeford Avenue

Downsview, Ontario

M3H 1K4 Canada

FAX: (416) 633-3010

Printed in the United States of America by the Royal Fireworks
Press of Unionville, New York.

ACKNOWLEDGMENTS

It was Tom Kemnitz of Trillium Press who suggested that my article *The Most Important Problem in Education is to Come to Terms with Values* should be updated and republished as a short book. Unfortunately, the article was itself a summary—which should have been included in my 1977 book *Education, Values and Society*—in order to draw the book together around its title: for the 10 years it had been in preparation it had been known as *Objectives in Education*. I changed the title at the last minute—when it dawned on me what were the central issues. But the summary highlighting those issues—and the evidence for them—was written only after the book had been published—and given a still more relevant title. Updating that article to include relevant research conducted since 1976 has taken much longer than either Tom or I envisaged. This was partly because almost the same process recurred. What now emerged was that, to come to terms with values, we will have to develop new arrangements to manage public provision in such a way as to achieve its manifest goals effectively and, in particular, to cater for diversity. I, therefore, found myself attempting to write a summary of yet another book—a book which, this time, has yet to be written. As a result, I have, once again, changed the title after I had what I thought was a final draft. This time the title has become *Managing the Educational System for Effective Schooling*. On this occasion, though, we *have* attempted to draw the concluding sections of the book together around the new title. This could not have been done without the assistance of my wife, Stanley Nisbet, Paul Myerscough, and Kate Houchin.

Actually, Stanley Nisbet has read several drafts of this book, made penetrating and helpful comments, noted endless typographical and grammatical errors, and engaged me in substantive discussion of educational and societal management arrangements. Bryan Dockrell, Wells Foshay, and Betty Adams have, over many years, encouraged the work on which the book is based, provoked arguments which have helped me to clarify my thinking, and commented on various drafts of this particular book.

Grover Young and Paquita McMichael have both read and commented on the book. Thanks are also due to Michael Fogarty who, as Director of the Economic and Social Research Institute in Dublin, promoted and encouraged much of the research on which the book is based and thus initiated a train of activities without which the book could never have come into being.

Dan Tanner's assistance in assembling—at Rutgers University—a collection of early American Progressive Education writings and drawing my attention to relevant contributions was invaluable. It was he, too, who introduced me to Robinson's thesis and Popkewitz's articles. Angela Fraley not only shared her library of Progressive Education reprints, but also visited Teachers College and other libraries in order to obtain copies of documents to which I would otherwise not have had access. I am aware that Dan, Angela, and Wells are all disappointed that I still do not see in American Progressive Education writing what they would like me to see ... but I can only respond that I am disappointed that they do not hear me saying something that is, as far as I can see, not present in these writings! These mild mutual recriminations are not without wider significance: They bear directly on the question of why the practices of those teachers who have successfully nurtured high-level competencies over the past century have not diffused more widely through the educational system.

On another level, I am deeply indebted to Leslie Smith for inviting me to prepare a starter paper—and subsequent response—for the British Psychological Society's **Education Section Review**'s *Open Dialogue* on the implications of the value-based nature of competence. This led some of the commentators—especially Peter Tomlinson and Angus Gellatly—to take me to task for not having paid sufficient attention to the latent functions of education. I have attempted to remedy this oversight in Chapter 7 of this book. I am, however, particularly pleased to be able to acknowledge the value of this open dialogue because—as is emphasized in Chapter 10—it seems to me that we need more open debate between positions to advance understanding.

PREFACE

This book summarizes more than a quarter of a century's intermittently sustained research into the evaluation and improvement of educational provision. It is a progress report which adds another 15 years' work to a summary of what was, even after the first decade, described as "the most thorough evaluation of the educational system ever undertaken." The intervening years have taken us even deeper into uncharted territory. When we embarked on this journey it never crossed our minds that we would find ourselves arguing—indeed demonstrating—that appropriate beliefs about society and how it works are, in modern society, crucial determinants of competent behavior. Still less did we expect to find ourselves saying that it is an essential part of everyone's job—and specifically teachers' jobs—to study and seek to influence these wider societal processes so that we can do our jobs—as laid down in our job descriptions—effectively. Never did it cross our minds that we would find ourselves saying that new forms of bureaucracy and democracy are crucial to the widespread introduction of effective education. At the time, we thought that if only we could describe goals, provide the necessary understanding of educational processes, and generate the tools required to run those programs we would have done all that was necessary. How innocent we were!

At one level, this book is addressed to lecturers in colleges of education, educational policy makers, teachers, and student teachers. But, at other levels, it has implications for the role which psychology is expected to play in teacher education, the teaching of psychology, and the organization of social research more generally.

As far as teacher education is concerned, the book demonstrates very clearly that teachers do not just teach *subjects*. They are also expected to nurture (but often stunt) generic competencies—like initiative, the ability to communicate, and the ability to understand and influence society. If they are to do this effectively, they will need to understand the nature of these qualities and how they are to be fostered and assessed. Thus (albeit sadly neglected areas of) developmental psychology and psychometrics are directly relevant to their work. Teachers also participate—and need to participate more—in the management of their schools and the educational system as a whole. In other words, (again a sadly neglected area of) organizational psychology is directly, indeed crucially, relevant to their effectiveness. It is important to understand that what this means is that, unless teachers are expected to engage in these societal management activities *as an integral part of their jobs*—and not just as citizens—*they will be unable to perform their classroom teaching effectively.*

Just as the book highlights new roles for teachers and neglected determinants of teacher competence, so it highlights new roles for psychologists. It therefore has major implications for the undergraduate teaching of psychology, the images of themselves that psychologists are to be encouraged to develop, and the images that others are encouraged to develop of them. The book heavily underscores the need for new understandings in the area of developmental psychology and psychometrics. But, perhaps more importantly, it illustrates the application of organizational psychology to the management of society as an organization—the importance of clarifying the goals of public provision, the methods to be used to reach them, the barriers to the effective operation of the delivery systems, and the structures of participation, supervision, and staff appraisal that are required for effective public provision. More generally, it illustrates the roles of evaluation and the evaluator. As a result, it has implications for all who are responsible for the training of psychologists and especially for those who will embark on, or commission, psychological and social research.

CONTENTS

CHAPTER 1

OVERVIEW

The broad aim of this book is to show that there are hidden barriers to achieving widely agreed goals of education and to clarify the— often surprising—steps that are required if these goals are to be achieved.

The book begins, in Chapter 2, by summarizing evidence showing that there is widespread agreement among teachers, pupils, parents and employers that the main goal of education should be to foster such qualities as initiative, problem-solving ability, the ability to work with others, and the ability to understand and influence society.

The research summarized in Chapter 3 indicates that these are indeed the qualities required for effective behavior in the workplace, the community, the home, and in civic affairs. Of wider significance is their necessity in tackling the difficult environmental, social, and economic problems facing our society.

Chapter 4 summarizes some of our work on the nature of high-level competence. It emerges that the qualities which make for competence are best thought of as motivational dispositions. Effective behavior requires a large number of cumulative and substitutable, self-motivated, components of competence. These include the ability to think about ways of avoiding or overcoming unanticipated problems, the ability to motivate other people, and the ability to understand, and contribute to the development of, organizational and political systems.

Chapter 5 shows that, far from fostering desirable competencies, the effects of most schooling are socially dysfunctional. The educational system encourages counter-productive beliefs and attitudes, and leads to the promotion of those who are best able to present themselves as others would like to see them.

Chapter 6 investigates how effective parents, teachers, and managers nurture high-level competencies. It emerges that, amongst other things, they identify each individual's motives and incipient talents and then create *developmental environments* in which those concerned can practice and develop high-level competencies while carrying out activities they care about.

In addition to emphasizing the need for tools to help teachers think about the individual development of their pupils, Chapter 7 documents more problematic barriers to the achievement of educational goals in schools. These include:

what happens in schools is determined, not by the educational priorities of teachers, pupils, or parents, but by what is assessed in the credentialling process. It follows that, if schools are to foster high-level competencies, their assessment must be included in the certification process. Unfortunately, because high-level competencies are inseparable from values, this creates a host of dilemmas.

in fostering high-level competencies, teachers need to both influence the values and political beliefs of their pupils, and identify and harness their existing values. As a society, we are ambivalent about teachers doing either of these things.

One way of side-stepping some of the dilemmas posed by the value-laden nature of high-level competencies would be to offer parents and pupils a choice between a wide range of educational programs explicitly and effectively directed toward different goals.

Unfortunately, this "solution" creates further difficulties:

(a) there is a lack of the information which would be needed by parents and pupils to make an informed choice between different types of programs.

(b) there is a fear that, if different pupils were treated in different ways, some would get a better deal than others.

One way of overcoming these problems would involve those who manage education developing a range of alternatives designed to meet the needs of a cross-section of the population.

2

The quality of each option would need to be monitored, and information on the personal and social, short and long term, consequences of each collected and fed outward to the public (instead of upward through a bureaucratic hierarchy to elected representatives). The crucial importance of the decisions to be taken regarding the collection and dissemination of this information would mean that there would need to be open supervision of the decision-taking process.

Public servants need to be more accountable for innovative behavior and decisions taken in the interests of the public. However, before we can develop appropriate staff appraisal procedures, it will be necessary to recognize and dispel the idea that public servants are functionaries whose job it is to carry out the prescriptions of elected representatives.

The observations recorded thus far point to the conclusion that the reform of education has proved difficult because it is intimately bound up with the reform of government and society and especially of the public sector management system. In Chapters 8 and 9, two key components of the required system are discussed. These are, first, new arrangements to create a climate of innovation in schools, and, second, a new interface with the public.

The crucial change needed in the internal operation of the educational system is the creation of a climate of concern with innovation. This requires a structure, and time set aside, for "parallel organization" activity. Kanter gives this label to activities which are carried out alongside the hierarchically-organized day-to-day executory functions on which people currently concentrate most of their attention. Innovative activity requires a "flat," non-hierarchical, structure which enables those with ideas to obtain direct access to those who control the release of resources, and which facilitates the formation of task groups to tackle emergent projects. Teachers must develop a wider role, influencing the social constraints (such as the expectations of parents and administrators) which restrict their activities in the classroom. Finally, the effective execution of parallel organiza-

3

tion activity will require that the educational system is provided with access to a much better R&D structure. Only this can produce the concepts, tools, and organizational arrangements needed to expose and overcome the deep-seated barriers to effective education.

The arrangements just described are almost completely at odds with the widely held assumption that progress in education is to be made through governmental prescription of goals and the means to their achievement, and the use of tests to gauge their attainment.

Equally fundamental changes are required in the management of the educational system and its interface with the public. For more than 50 years, public servants have failed to act on information which demonstrates the failure of the educational system to achieve its goals effectively. Chapter 9 deals with the role of the public servant in the management of education. It argues that, in order to ensure that information is acted upon in the public interest, public servants' behavior should be exposed to public scrutiny and their actions monitored for innovation and effectiveness.

To monitor and assist the work of teachers and other public servants, it is proposed that a fluid, network-based, supervisory structure be established. The "monitoring" groups would consist of those with a relevant interest—we might envisage a group made up of parents, members of the local community, teachers and researchers. Since the activities of any one teacher must be related to those of other teachers in the school, and in turn to those in other schools in the community and the country generally, there is a clear need for a network of linked groups as well as links via the media and research.

The establishment of any network-based supervisory structure would involve finding ways of encouraging more people to play an active part in the management of society. Chapter 9 goes on to suggest that the solution to this problem lies in recognizing that public-sector activities are themselves wealth-creating, so that participation in their management merits remuneration.

4

While this is a highly practical book, its main contribution is to advance **understanding**. Indeed, its main conclusion is that the development of the understandings, organizational arrangements, and tools required for the effective management of our society is heavily dependent on investment in innovative, policy-relevant, social research. Unfortunately, because the management of research rests in the hands of those who lack the very competencies the book is primarily concerned with, the practice and supervision of research needs to change dramatically. The required understandings and arrangements are discussed in Chapter 10. It emerges that the requisite research is an adventurous and problem-driven activity. Also that research which advances basic understanding, and contributes to the invention and development of new administrative and assessment tools can only be carried out in the context of action: it is, for example, not possible to develop valid measures of high-level competencies without changing schoolroom practice, but classroom processes will not change until we have means of giving pupils and teachers credit for alternative outcomes.

Any attempt to change the state of education faces a tissue of problems none of which can be tackled on its own and most of which pose Catch 22s. Thus classroom processes cannot be improved without better measures of their outcomes, the development of the tools needed to administer them, new concepts of management, and reform of the interface between schools and society. Such change in turn demands change in social practice. Social change can occur only if we develop better concepts of competence, better staff appraisal systems, and better institutional arrangements. Yet the research for these developments can not be carried out without the improved organizational arrangements which it is the very object of the research itself to develop.

What these observations mean is that the need is for systems analysis followed by multiple developments which will contribute to multi-pronged intervention designed to counteract the system's tendency to negate the effects of single interventions. The need is for experimental and carefully evaluated systemic intervention grounded in a high-level understanding of systems processes, not for system-wide intervention based in common sense.

It would not be appropriate to conclude this overview without noting the wider significance of the developments required to improve the educational system. Our society is in great need of management structures which will facilitate urgent innovative action to tackle the current environmental, financial, and public sector management crises. The evolution of an effective educational system would lead to the development of the competencies required to promote the development of such a system. But, more specifically, the development of an effective educational management system would contribute directly to the evolution of more effective ways of running society.

PART I

EDUCATIONAL GOALS:
THEIR NATURE AND ACHIEVEMENT—
AND THE REASONS FOR THEIR NEGLECT

CHAPTER 2

EDUCATION HAS CENTRALLY TO DO WITH VALUES

As a basis around which to organize a discussion of educational goals and objectives, and in order to establish criteria against which to evaluate the educational system, we began, in the mid 60s in England and Wales, to undertake what became a series of studies of parents', teachers', pupils', ex-pupils', employees', and employers' priorities in education.[2.1] These surveys have now been replicated (or parallel data have been collected) by researchers in the United States and many other countries such as the Republic of Ireland, Belgium, Scotland and France.[2.2]

Respondents were asked how important they thought each of a number of possible educational goals or objectives were. Each of the objectives had been stressed by one group or another in the exploratory and pilot stages of the surveys. It should be noted that those who answered our questions were able, if they so wished, to rate some (or none) of the objectives as "Very Important." This procedure differed in two major ways from that adopted by Goodlad[2.3] in America. Goodlad's first obtained ratings of the importance attached to each of four goal *areas*— "academic" (including critical thinking as well as basic skills), "vocational," "social and civic" (relating to preparation for entry into a complex society), and "personal" (relating to the development of individual responsibility, self-confidence, creativity, and thinking for oneself). This difference in methodology could lead to different conclusions because we found that some goals within each domain were rated "very important" while others were not. Nevertheless, Goodlad did find that pupils, parents, and teachers rated *all four* areas "very important." He declared "most parents want their children to have it all." However he then went on to ask his respondents to select the single goal area they believed to be *most* important. It was on their responses to this forced-choice question that he based the discussions in the later chapters of his book. These proceed on the assumption that most clients of the educational system want schools to focus mainly on "academic" goals. This is, most emphatically, *not* supported by our data. Goodlad's very different conclusions therefore stem, in part, from differences in methodology. Our own conclusions are much closer to those of Flanagan[2.4] and Johnston and Bachman.[2.5]

Table 2.1 shows the objectives arranged in order of the importance that was assigned to them by Irish, adolescent boys.[2.6] Note the first item. It reads "Ensure that you leave school confident, willing, and able to take the initiative in introducing changes." Readers who believe that schools should *not* be seeking to foster the abilities and understandings required to bring about social change should be challenged by these data. In the eyes of the majority of these clients of the educational system, the *primary* objective of education is to foster the qualities required

---

KEY TO SHADING IN CHARTS

Self-Initiated Competencies and Qualities of Character

Guidance

Information which can be used in everyday jobs and lives

Academic knowledge content

Prescriptive Oughts

Activity Methods, mostly directed towards developing Self-initiated Competences

Emotional Feelings at the time

9

TABLE 2.1

Importance of Objectives: Boys.

Percentages of boys rating each objective "Very Important."

1. Ensure that you leave school confident, willing and able to take the initiative in introducing changes.
2. Encourage you to be independent and able to stand on your own feet.
3. Help you to do as well as possible in external examinations like the Intermediate, Leaving, Group Certificate.
4. Have outside speakers about careers and other educational topics.
5. Ensure that you know how to apply the facts and techniques you have learned to new problems.
6. Tell you about different sorts of jobs and careers so that you can decide what you want to do.
7. Have discussion lessons in which you would discuss things and put forward your point of view.
8. Help you to develop your character and personality.
9. Help you to understand the implications and responsibilities of marriage.
10. Ensure that you leave school intent on being master of your destiny.
11. Encourage friendships between boys and girls by, for example, running co-educational hobbies and social clubs.
12. Ensure that you can speak well and put what you want to say into words easily.
13. Make sure that you are able to read and study on your own.
14. Help you think out what you really want to achieve in life.
15. Encourage you to have opinions of your own.
16. Provide you with sex education in the school.
17. Advise parents to give sex education to their children.
18. Teach you things that will be of direct use to you when you start work in your job or career.
19. Give you experience of taking responsibility.
20. Make sure that you get an education that is so interesting, useful and enjoyable that you will be keen to continue your education in adult life.
21. Make sure that you get a thorough religious education.
22. Take you on visits to factories or offices or other places to see the different sorts of jobs there are and what work is like.
23. Give you information about the courses of Further and Higher education that are open to you.
24. Make sure that you really enjoy the lessons.
25. Run clubs and societies (e.g. sports, hobbies, social and youth clubs) for pupils out of school hours.

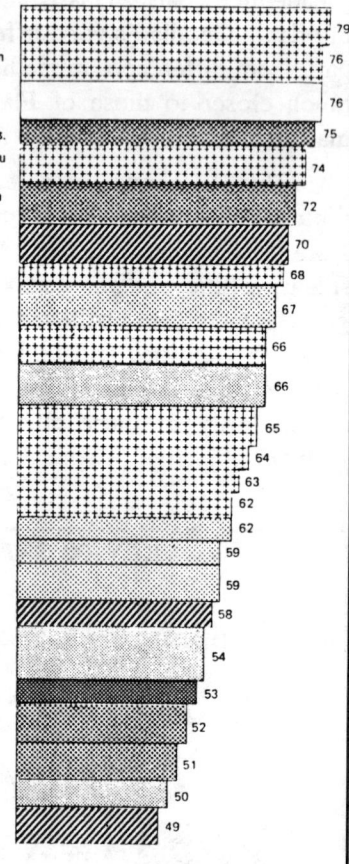

Item	%
1	79
2	76
3	76
4	75
5	74
6	72
7	70
8	68
9	67
10	66
11	66
12	65
13	64
14	63
15	62
16	62
17	59
18	59
19	58
20	54
21	53
22	52
23	51
24	50
25	49

TABLE 2.1 Contd.

26. Educational visits in connection with your subjects – such as to see chemical plants, museums and theatres. 48
27. Give you a say in how the school is run. 48
28. Make sure you are confident and at ease when dealing with people. 46
29. Ensure that you can express yourself clearly in writing. 45
30. Help you to develop a considerate attitude towards other people. 45
31. Make sure you go out into the world determined to make Ireland a better place in which to live. 44
32. Teach you about what is right and wrong. 44
33. Provide facilities for pupils to do their homework at school. 43
34. Help you to get on with other people. 41
35. Encourage you to have a good time. 40
36. Help you to take an interest in and to understand what is going on in the world now. 39
37. Introduce you to new subjects, e.g. philosophy, sociology, archaeology etc. 38
38. Encourage you to have a sense of duty towards the community 36
39. Make sure that you leave school aware of the prolonged struggle for Irish freedom and determined to uphold the ideals which inspired it. 33
40. Ensure that you feel confident and at ease when dealing with figures and numbers. 33
41. Enable you to develop an interest in subjects other than those studied for examinations. 33
42. Teach you about a wide range of cultures and philosophies so that your own can be seen to be only one of many. 33
43. Have Project work, that is work in which you have to make something or do some investigation and write it up. 28
44. Make sure you have opportunities to give short lectures and talks to the rest of your class. 27
45. Ensure that you are aware of aspects of school subjects which you do not have to know for the examinations. 27
46. Teach you about bringing up children, home repairs, decorating and so on. 27
47. Take you on holidays in this country or abroad. 25
48. Run courses for adults as well as young people. 24
49. Have rules about the clothes and hairstyles you may wear in school. 14
50. Have rules about the sort of things you may do outside of school hours. 8

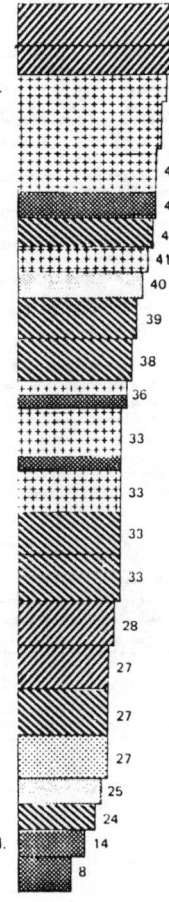

11

TABLE 2.2

Importance of Objectives: Girls.

Percentages of girls rating each objective "Very Important."

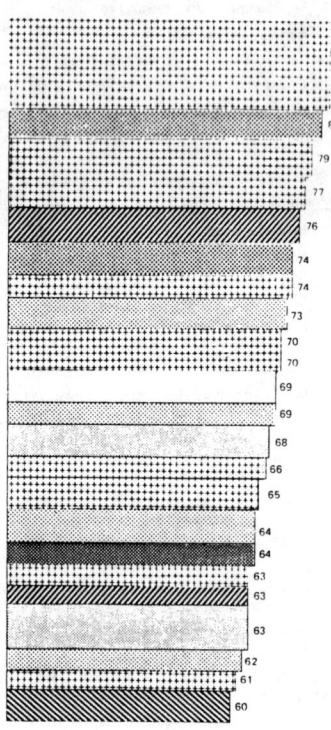

1. Ensure that you leave school confident, willing and able to take the initiative in introducing changes. — 85
2. Encourage you to be independent and able to stand on your own feet. — 82
3. Help you to develop your character and personality. — 81
4. Have outside speakers about careers and other educational topics. — 81
5. Ensure that you know how to apply the facts and techniques you have learned to new problems. — 79
6. Ensure that you can speak well and put what you want to say into words easily. — 77
7. Have discussion lessons in which you would discuss things and put forward your point of view. — 76
8. Tell you about different sorts of jobs and careers so that you can decide what you want to do. — 74
9. Encourage you to have opinions of your own. — 74
10. Help you to understand the implications and responsibilities of marriage. — 73
11. Make sure that you are able to read and study on your own. — 70
12. Help you to think out what you really want to achieve in life. — 70
13. Help you to do as well as possible in external examinations like the Intermediate, Leaving, Group Certificate. — 69
14. Advise parents to give sex education to their children. — 69
15. Encourage friendships between boys and girls, for example, by running co-educational hobbies and social clubs. — 68
16. Help you to develop a considerate attitude towards other people. — 66
17. Ensure that you leave school intent on being master of your destiny. — 65
18. Teach you things that will be of direct use to you when you start work in your job or career. — 64
19. Make sure that you get a thorough religious education. — 64
20. Make sure you are confident and at ease when dealing with people. — 63
21. Give you experience of taking responsibility. — 63
22. Make sure that you get an education that is so interesting, useful and enjoyable that you will be keen to continue your education in adult life. — 63
23. Provide you with sex education in the school. — 62
24. Help you to get on with other people. — 61
25. Help you to take an interest in and to understand what is going on in the world now. — 60

12

TABLE 2.2 Contd.

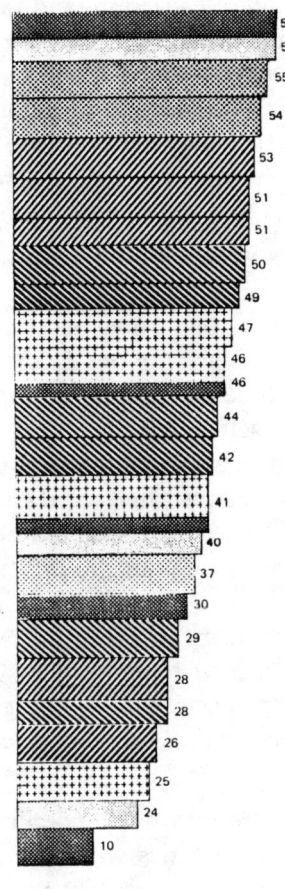

26. Teach you about what is right and wrong. — 59
27. Make sure that you really enjoy the lesson. — 59
28. Give you information about the courses of Further and Higher education that are open to you. — 55
29. Take you on visits to factories or offices or other places to see the different sorts of jobs there are and what work is like. — 54
30. Educational visits in connection with your subjects — such as to see chemical plants, museums and theatres. — 53
31. Run clubs and societies (e.g. sports, hobbies, social and youth clubs) for pupils out of school hours. — 51
32. Give you a say in how the school is run. — 51
33. Introduce you to new subjects, e.g. philosophy, sociology, archaeology etc. — 50
34. Provide facilities for pupils to do their homework at school. — 49
35. Make sure you go out in the world determined to make Ireland a better place in which to live. — 47
36. Ensure that you can express yourself clearly in writing. — 46
37. Encourage you to have a sense of duty towards the community. — 46
38. Teach you about a wide range of cultures and philosophies so that your own can be seen to be only one of many. — 44
39. Enable you to develop an interest in subjects other than those studied for examinations. — 42
40. Make sure that you leave school aware of the prolonged struggle for Irish freedom and determined to uphold the ideals which inspired it. — 41
41. Encourage you to have a good time. — 40
42. Teach you about bringing up children, home repairs, decorating and so on. — 37
43. Have rules about the clothes and hairstyles you may wear in school. — 30
44. Ensure that you are aware of aspects of school subjects which you do not have to know for the examination. — 29
45. Have Project work, that is work in which you have to make something or do some investigation and write it up. — 28
46. Run courses for adults as well as young people. — 28
47. Make sure you have opportunities to give short lectures and talks to the rest of your class. — 26
48. Ensure that you feel confident and at ease when dealing with figures and numbers. — 25
49. Take you on holidays in this country or abroad. — 24
50. Have rules about the sort of things you may do outside of school hours. — 10

13

to bring about change. If one reflects for a moment on what these might be, one finds oneself thinking of qualities—like initiative, leadership, and the ability to intervene in political systems—which can only be practiced and displayed in the course of activities which are not characteristic of school tasks: in how many classrooms do pupils display the levels of commitment, energy, and collaboration in forward-looking activity which is conjured up by such a phrase?

There are several other objectives near the top of the pupils' lists which imply similar activities: independence of thought and behavior; applying what one has learned to new problems; making one's own observations; finding information for oneself; being master of one's destiny. One important characteristic of all of these qualities is that they involve a high degree of spontaneity and self-motivation. Yet one has the impression that these activities are rarely called for in schools—and, as we will see in a later chapter, that impression is amply supported by the available evidence. Instead, the activities which dominate most classrooms lead pupils to practice being docile, to tolerate boring and useless activities, and to be dependent rather than independent. They learn to expect to be told what to learn—and possibly to learn how to pretend to have learned what is put in front of them—instead of learning how to notice new problems, make their own observations, collect their own data, and think for themselves.

We may next underline the forward-looking nature of many of the qualities which the students thought it was important for schools to foster. The majority of them are saying that they want schools to help them to clarify their life goals and values and then enable them to develop the competencies which are required to achieve them effectively. Again, how many schools make a serious effort to satisfy such needs?

The items having to do with careers information and helping pupils to think out what they really want to achieve in life deserve special discussion. In addition to asking the pupils how important they thought each of the objectives in Tables 2.1 and

14

2.2 were, we also asked them how satisfied they were with what their school did to achieve each and how important they thought it was for their school to do more to achieve them. What then emerged was that the careers information and guidance objectives were perceived to be the most neglected and poorly attained of all the objectives that were considered to be very important.

This perception is entirely borne out by Flanagan's[2.7] American data: an enormous amount of time is lost, and a great deal of distress is caused, as people flounder around in the job market until they find a niche which taps their (previously unidentified) personal interests and talents. Guidance is one of the most important and neglected goals of education. Flanagan's data also shows that work is typically the first occasion which people have to discover **and develop** their true potentials. Bachman's[2.8] work at the Institute of Social Research, Michigan, likewise shows that 83% of young people said they had been better able to both identify and develop their talents at work compared with school. And Csikszentmihalyi and Le Fevre's[2.9] work shows that people's most important life satisfactions come from exercising personally important talents at the borders of their capability.

The interpretation to be placed on these data is, however, not necessarily the obvious one. It may be that, instead of *defining* a problem, the pupils have only *indicated the existence of a problem* by endorsing a widely canvassed possible **solution** to that problem. It is entirely possible that careers information and guidance would **not** solve the problem. Several observations support this contention. In the first place, the pupils involved in our own surveys did not find the careers guidance that they were given very helpful. Flanagan's[2.10] attempt to provide what appeared to be the required information by computer did not prove to be any more satisfactory. And the most expensive project ever commissioned by the Schools Council for Curriculum and Examinations in England and Wales failed to solve the problem.

If careers guidance does not solve the problem, perhaps its nature has been mis-defined. On reflection, how *could* any form of conventional **careers** guidance and information solve it? All occupational groups encompass a wide range of people who have very different motives and talents and who do very different things. Thus the psychological profession includes people who raise research funds, others who generate new ideas and ways of thinking about things, others who invent new ways of doing things, others who edit journals and magazines, others who lecture, others who write books, others who run companies, others who manage personnel within companies, some who study rats, some who study primitive people, some who study nervous systems, some who study organizational structures ... and so on. The same is true of other occupational groups. Consider panelbeaters. The group needs some members who are "good with customers," others who can take an idea and translate it into a workable prototype, others who negotiate the best deal for the group with management, and so on. It therefore seems that what students really mean when they say they want "careers guidance" is some means of identifying their latent motives and incipient talents, a means of linking such information to opportunities to develop those talents and test emergent hypotheses about what might tap their enthusiasm, some way of getting recognition for the talents thus developed, and assistance in finding ways of utilizing, further developing, and being rewarded for utilizing, those motives and talents in the workplace.

Reverting to our discussion of students' priorities in education, the next point to be noted is that their view of education is distinctly instrumental. They want schools to help them to develop qualities which would enable them to lead their lives effectively, to help them to obtain high grades and therefore get into high status courses or jobs, and to provide the guidance needed to help them to identify and develop talents which will be useful in the future and indicate ways in which it will be possible to further develop and capitalize upon those talents in the workplace. Relatively few of them think it is very important for schools to engage in cultural activities or to inculcate moral values in the more prescriptive way that is, for example, characteristic of many who advocate values education.[2.11]

16

There is one final, and very important, point to be highlighted from the pupils' responses. Students attach little importance to learning about aspects of school subjects which are not required for examination purposes (ie, aspects which do not contribute to obtaining high grades) or to studying non-examined academic subjects. These come in positions 45 and 41, respectively, in the boys' list. This discrepancy between the importance attached to grades and the perceived insignificance of the content, taken together with other information gleaned from our survey—such as the annoyance which pupils report if they are given lessons which are informative and enjoyable but without the syllabus on which they are graded—suggests that what they mean when they say—as they did in Goodlad's survey—that they want an academic education is that they want an education which confers good grades. It is not knowledge—or even academic skills—they seek. They want good grades because these control access to protected occupations and privileged positions in society. The knowledge on which the grades are based is of scant value in itself. Goodlad's data amply support this conclusion.

Interestingly enough, as we shall soon see more precisely (Table 2.3), this perception is almost shared by their teachers. Teachers do not even include getting pupils through examinations among their top 20 objectives. But they do not discriminate between the grades and the content on which they are based: both are equally important. In rather different ways, therefore, it seems that teachers and pupils spend most of their time working, against their will, toward goals which they do not consider to be of direct educational value. This seems to be the most likely explanation of the widely reported "lack of motivation" among pupils and demoralization among teachers.

It might be possible to reduce this tension if ways could be found to give pupils credit in the certification and placement process—which controls access to jobs and courses of further and higher education—for having developed the qualities which they themselves believe to be most important. This is, however, problematical. One reason for this is that most of the qualities which come high up on the pupils' lists involve values or can only be fostered and displayed while pupils are undertaking activities they care about (ie, value). Another reason is that any assessment of outcomes in this area would, in current circumstances, expose the inadequacy of the educational system.

Despite these difficulties, it would seem that if anything is to be done about the problems which confront the educational system, it will be necessary to find ways of giving pupils and teachers credit for having developed the kinds of quality which pupils (and parents) think are so important. If this is to be done, it will be necessary to assess value-laden qualities. This is something which our society has, in the past, been unwilling to do openly and it will therefore be necessary to explore the reasons why this has been the case and seek methods to overcome them. Failure to do so will mean that we will perpetuate both a dysfunctional educational system and inappropriate manpower policies.

Teachers' Views

Table 2.3 presents teachers' educational priorities. The list has a more prescriptive ring about it than the pupils' list. Whereas many pupils gave priority to developing qualities which were expansive, self-determined, self-motivated, forward-looking, adventurous, and open-ended, the teachers' priorities include fostering a sense of duty toward the community and teaching about what is right and wrong. Nevertheless, it also includes fostering independence and encouraging pupils to have opinions of their own. The kinds of activities that would be required if teachers were to achieve this kind of objective, would, like those required to achieve the goals at the top of the pupils' list, be a great deal more growth-enhancing than most of what—as we shall see—occupies most of the time of most pupils in most classrooms at the present time. The differences between the teachers' and the pupils' order of priorities, while important, should therefore not be exaggerated. There is a great deal of scope for teachers and pupils to move forward in a common enterprise.

TABLE 2.3

The Importance of Educational Objectives.

Percent of teachers saying each objective "Very Important" for "more academic" pupils.

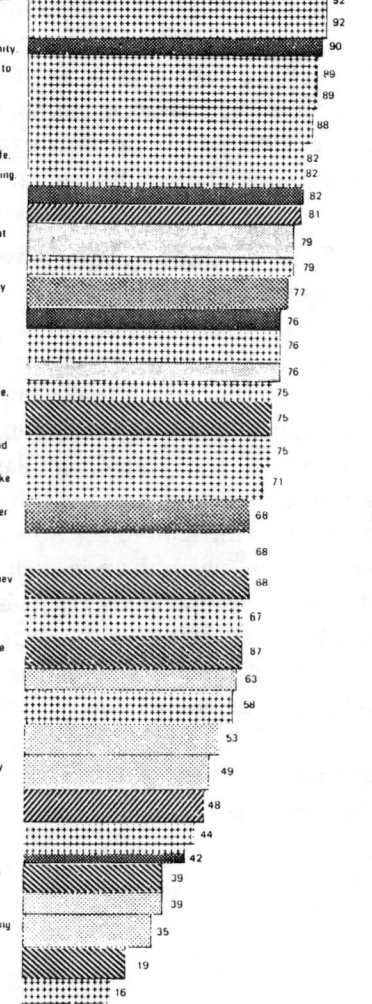

1. Help them to develop their characters and personalities.	93
2. Encourage pupils to be independent and to be able to stand on their own feet.	92
3. Make sure that they are able to read and study on their own.	92
4. Encourage them to have a sense of duty towards the community.	90
5. Ensure that all pupils can speak well and put what they want to say into words easily.	89
6. Encourage them to have opinions of their own.	89
7. Help them to develop a considerate attitude towards other people.	88
8. Help them to think out what they really want to achieve in life.	82
9. Ensure that all students can express themselves clearly in writing.	82
10. Teach them about what is right and wrong.	82
11. Give them experience of taking responsibility.	81
12. Make sure that they get edn. so inting. usefl. and enjoyable that they will continue as adult.*	79
13. Help them to get on with other people.	79
14. Tell them about different sorts of jobs and careers so that they can decide what they want to do.	77
15. Make sure they get a thorough religious education.	76
16. Ensure that they know how to apply the facts and techniques they have learned to new problems.	76
17. Make sure that they really enjoy the lesson.	76
18. Make sure they are confident and at ease in dealing with people.	75
19. Help them to take an interest in and to understand what is going on in the world now.	75
20. Make sure they go out in the world determined to make Ireland a better place in which to live.	75
21. Ensure that they leave school confident, willing and able to take the initiative in introducing changes.	71
22. Give them information about the courses of Further and Higher Education that are open to them.	68
23. Help them to do as well as possible in external examinations like the Intermediate, Group or Leaving Certificates.	68
24. Ensure that they are aware of aspects of your subject which they do not have to know for the examinations.	68
25. Ensure that they can formulate hypotheses, seek evidence and reason logically.	67
26. Enable them to develop an interest in subjects other than those studied for examinations.	67
27. Advise parents to give sex education to their children.	63
28. Ensure that they leave school intent on being masters of their destinies.	58
29. Help them to understand the implications and responsibilities of marriage.	53
30. Teach them things that will be of direct use to them when they start work in their jobs or careers.	49
31. Run clubs and societies (e.g. sports, hobbies, social and youth clubs) for pupils out of school hours.	48
32. Ensure that all pupils feel at home with figures and numbers.	44
33. Irish freedom*	42
34. Teach them about a wide range of cultures and philosophies so that their own can be seen to be one of many	39
35. Provide the pupils with sex education in the school.	39
36. Teach them about bringing up children, home repairs, decorating and so on.	35
37. Introduce them to new subjects e.g. philosophy, sociology, archaeology etc.	19
38. Teach them to be sceptical, that is to take little on trust.	16
39. Encourage them to have a good time.	13

*These two items have been abbreviated from the items on the questionnaire which read:

"Make sure that they get an education that is so interesting, useful and enjoyable that they will be keen to continue their formal education in adult life".

"Ensure that they are aware of the prolonged struggle for Irish freedom and are determined to uphold the ideals which inspired it."

Weighted base (= 100%) All teachers rating objectives for "more academic" pupils: 612.

In connection with our earlier discussion of the discrepancy between the importance which pupils attached to grades and the perceived unimportance of the content on which those grades are based, it is significant that getting pupils through examinations comes down in position 23 in the teachers' order of priorities, but is immediately followed by content. Thus, while pupils think that getting high grades is important, but that the content on which they are based is unimportant, teachers do not even think that getting pupils through examinations is all that important compared with other objectives. The irony is that, as we will see, it is the objective which claims the lion's share of their attention.

Table 2.4 shows comparative data obtained in earlier British Surveys for pupils, ex-pupils, and parents on the one hand and teachers and headmasters on the other.[2.12] What these data show is that there are major discrepancies between the first three groups and the others in the importance attached to many of the instrumental goals of education. These include high scores on achievement tests, careers guidance, and things of direct use in a job or career, although the difference is greatest on the careers items. It is difficult to see how *any* real progress can be made in a climate in which there is such a marked conflict in perceptions of what education is about. It is also significant that there is, in this table, *no* evidence to support the view, often expressed by teachers, that pupils will change their minds as they grow up, get jobs, and become parents. There is *no* evidence that pupils will later regret not paying attention to some of the more social and cultural goals that teachers and head teachers are more likely to consider important.

TABLE 2.4

Proportions of 15-year-old leavers, their parents and teachers saying that various school objectives were very important.

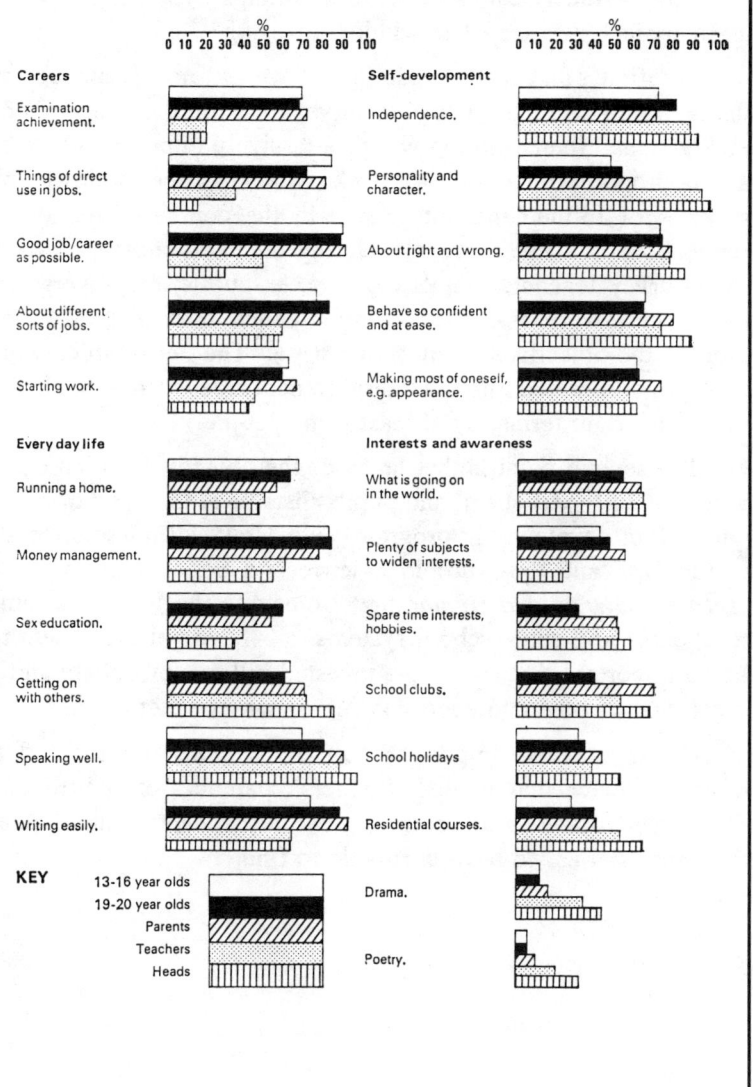

KEY
- 13-16 year olds
- 19-20 year olds
- Parents
- Teachers
- Heads

The Validity of the Data

How seriously can we take these ratings by teachers, pupils and parents? Are they just window dressing?

The first point to be made is that we did not dream up the items which were used in our surveys out of the blue. They emerged, and their wording was progressively improved, through a long program of exploratory work (which has been followed by a series of refinements introduced in the course of numerous replications of these surveys). During the exploratory phases of each survey teachers, pupils, parents, ex-pupils, employers and employees, were asked, in an open-ended manner, what they thought the objectives of education were. The items which were finally incorporated into the interview schedules were articulated, in no uncertain terms, by at least some people.[2.13]

The second point is that many of the objectives which came at the top of the teachers' and pupils' lists lie at the heart of many curriculum development programs like *Man: A Course of Study* in the U.S. and the Nutfield Science and Schools Council *Integrated Science and Humanities* Projects in the U.K.[2.14] Some teachers— and some school systems[2.15]—have believed them to be so important that they have invested billions of dollars and a great deal of time and energy trying to achieve them.

But much more important than any response of this sort is direct evidence that pupils', teachers', parents', ex-pupils' and employers' opinions are correct. The next chapter summarizes such material as we have been able to find.

CHAPTER 3

THE COMPETENCIES REQUIRED AT WORK AND IN SOCIETY

In an attempt to find out whether the teachers', pupils', parents', and ex-pupils' opinions on the goals of education that were discussed in the last chapter were correct, we reviewed the available literature on the competencies required at work and in society.[3.1] This chapter briefly summarizes some of the results.

The Qualities Required at Work

Klemp, Munger and Spencer[3.2] and I[3.3] have shown (Table 3.1) that more effective managers are distinguished from their less effective peers by their greater tendency to do such things as think about and develop the talents of their subordinates, move their subordinates into positions in which they can capitalize on their talents and have their contributions recognized by their organizations, listen to what lies behind what people say, and do something about it, reflect on the workings of their organizations and intervene effectively in them, analyze the workings of the wider social system around their organizations and orchestrate effective inter-organizational activity to influence such wider constraints. Our work also shows that the willingness and the ability to do the things which have just been mentioned is rare among American and British managers but is much more common in Singapore and Japan.[3.4]

Managerial competence is by no means the only area of competence which has been analyzed. Thus Raven and Dolphin[3.5] studied a cross-section of employees in a wide variety of organizations ranging from the civil service, through banks and offices, to large factories. The qualities required to deal with the problems which plagued these organizations were the qualities which were emphasized by the parents, teachers, and pupils whose views were reported in the previous chapter. However, although employers were often anxious to do so, they frequently failed to develop and utilize the wide variety of values, talents, and competencies which were available in their workforce. This was largely because they lacked constructs for thinking about the relevant talents and abilities, how to develop them, and how to utilize them. In particular, they lacked means of assessing them.

Research has also been carried out among construction site workers,[3.6] bus drivers,[3.7] nurses,[3.8] small businessmen,[3.9] social workers,[3.10] architects,[3.11] pharmacists,[3.12] town planners,[3.13] civil servants,[3.14] doctors,[3.15] scientists,[3.16] engineers,[3.17] and politicians.[3.18] Only one or two further examples can be dis-

---

TABLE 3.1

Competencies of More Effective Officers

- Takes initiative: initiates new activities, communication, proposals; exhibits resourcefulness, persistence in the face of obstacles.
- Sets goals and reconsiders and redefines them.
- Coaches, by setting example and sharing information, feelings, and thought processes.
- Influences: by persuasion, mustering arguments, building political coalitions, making others feel strong.
- Conceptualizes, analyzes, and finds new ways of thinking about things.
- Builds teams, acts to promote cooperation and team work.
- Provides feedback to enable others to monitor their own performance. Helps them analyze problems and develop strategies for tackling them.
- Provides rewards and official recognition for contributions.
- Controls impulses, especially annoyance. Avoids snap decisions based on incomplete evidence.
- Plans and organizes, including "Domain Planning."
- Delegates.
- Optimizes: analyzes the capacity of individuals and resources and requirements of a job, matches the two and fully utilizes the resources available.
- Monitors own behavior and that of others.
- Resolves conflicts.
- Listens actively and initiates opportunities to give others a chance to talk.
- Has accurate empathy; makes explicit unexpressed thoughts and feelings of others.
- Helps.

cussed here. Table 3.2 shows the competencies which Flanagan and Burns[3.19] found to distinguish more from less effective machine operatives. Their results have been confirmed more recently in a study conducted by the Industrial Training Research Unit in Great Britain.[3.20] We ourselves[3.21] found that what 20-year-olds who had been "drop-outs" from school at 15 years of age liked about their job was the variety, the opportunity to take initiative, the opportunity to make the most of themselves, and the opportunity to develop and use their talents in ways which had not been possible at school. They also liked the fact that they did not, at work, have to do the same thing all the time and do things they could not do. It emerges that work—even for this early-leaving group—is anything but the soul-destroying activity which many teachers take it to be. Grannis[3.22] and Bachman *et al*[3.23] obtained confirmatory results in the US.

Finally, it is, perhaps, particularly appropriate in a book like this to list (in Table 3.3) some of the qualities which have been found to distinguish more from less effective school teachers.[3.24]

Taken as a whole, these data convincingly demonstrate that parents, teachers, pupils and employers are right to say that the educational system should be primarily concerned with fostering such qualities as initiative, the ability to make one's own observations, the competencies required to identify and solve problems, the ability to work with others, leadership, and the ability to understand and influence the workings of society.

TABLE 3.2

Competencies Distinguishing between More and Less Effective Machine Operatives.

- Dependability.
- Accuracy of Reporting.
- Tendency to respond to the needs of the situation without having to be given instructions.
- Ability to get on with others.
- Responsibility

TABLE 3.3

Competencies Distinguishing between More and Less Effective School Teachers.

- The ability to work with parents to establish community support networks which allow parents to create developmental environments for their children.
- The capacity to convince community members of the desirability of individualized, competence-oriented educational programs of growth in schools.
- The willingness and the ability to analyze the role which sociological forces play in determining what happens in schools, and the ability to harness these sociological forces to push them in the direction in which they wish to go.
- The ability to handle the political problems which arise when pupils are encouraged to develop the capacities required to tackle pressing social problems such as pollution.
- The ability to identify the talents of all their pupils and to create group and individual educational processes which enable all children to develop their unique patterns of competence.
- The ability to evolve, in cooperation with other teachers, their own understanding of how growth is to be promoted and how to gain control over the wider constraints on education—instead of waiting for authority to tell them what to do.

Civic Competence

But these are not the most important insights into the competencies to be fostered by the educational system which have emerged from our work.

Some 20 years ago, I was offered an opportunity to study "values, attitudes and institutional structures associated with economic and social development" in the Republic of Ireland. I approached my task, as a psychologist would, with the idea of finding out how important such qualities as "*need* achievement," "leadership," and "creativity" might be. I thought I might get a feel for how important such qualities were by speaking to people who had a range of different sorts of jobs and asking them to tell me something about their jobs and their lives. When they started to get excited about some problem they had, I would ask them what they could do about it.

To my surprise they, one after another, said "There's nothing I can do about it; the government must do it." My first reaction to this was one of shock. I thought "What has happened to their initiative, leadership, and ability to persuade others to help them to do something about their problems?" At first I did not realize that what people were actually saying related directly to my interest in competence and that it would lead to a re-interpretation of concepts like leadership. However, what they were saying did seem important—even if I did not quite know why—and it therefore seemed relevant to document their views more systematically. For this reason, and because we were in the fortunate position of not having to explain precisely why we were collecting particular data before we did so, we were able to undertake a number of studies of civic and political culture and political socialization.[3.25]

While this work was in hand, two things happened.

Firstly, I realized that what I had discovered was that people's behavior is not *mainly* determined by such qualities as "initiative," *need* Achievement, or *need* Power, but by their beliefs about society, how it works, and their place in it. Or, rather, that whether people will take a leadership role or display initiative is markedly influenced by these beliefs and perceptions. Appropriate social and political beliefs are therefore key psychological components in the cluster of activities that we refer to when we use terms like initiative and leadership.

Secondly, I, once again, discovered that cumulated public opinion is a good guide to the truth. An economist introduced me to some statistics which showed that 45% of GNP is, in all the countries of the European Community, spent directly by their governments. It turns out that even this does not include the spending of the nationalized industries or local government. When these are added on the figure rises to 65%. And this still does not include the effects of grant and levy schemes, planning legislation, health and safety legislation, or requirements that firms provide pensions—which are all designed to lead people to spend much more of their "own" money in ways determined by government. Including these brings the total to some 75%. So it *was* necessary—as my informants said—for the government to tackle *their* problems. Their task then became to influence the government ... but they jibbed at that—and for rational—but inadequate—reasons which do not need to be discussed here.[3.26]

I finally realized the true import of these observations nearly 15 years later, when I was working on the text of *Competence in Modern Society*. What I then found myself saying was that competence in modern society has almost more than anything else to do with the willingness and the ability to gain control over the wider social and political forces which come from outside one's job, but which primarily determine what one *can* do in it. So beliefs about the meaning and implications of such terms as "democracy," "participation," "management" and "citizenship" turn out to be central to competence.

It may be thought that these observations do not apply to the United States where government, it is often said, plays a less significant role. However, when visiting the United States, I have repeatedly found that what look like independent organizations have either been brought into being by governmental legislation (like much insurance and medical schemes and much psychological assessment), or are somehow or other dependent on government money—like the research units which are dependent on defense or education contracts and the interventions in agricultural prices and production. I suspect that, if a careful study were made, the results would be not too different from those we have obtained in Europe. Of course, it is always possible to argue about such things as how much control governments really have over such things as how transfer payments— money supposedly taken from the rich and given to the poor—are actually spent. But, whatever the room for argument, the conclusion that governments play a major role in the management of modern societies is indisputable.

Actually, the importance of finding better ways of managing modern society is more serious than even these observations suggest.

In another attempt to try to decide which competencies it is most important for schools to foster, we modified and replicated a study which had previously been carried out by Flanagan and Russ-Eft[3.27] in the United States. We first undertook a quality-of-life survey to identify the problems which people had in leading their lives as they would have liked. Then we studied what competencies and understandings they would need if they were to tackle these problems effectively.

What we found was that people **are** dissatisfied with the quality of their consumer goods. They are still more dissatisfied with the quality of the environments in which they live and work. But they are **most** dissatisfied with their *relationships* with politicians and public servants. It turns out that this is because these politicians and public servants govern the quality of people's lives by controlling health services, welfare services, education services, manpower policy, income distributions, prices, and international trade (including trade with the Third World). But it is not the policies themselves that are the **main** problem (important though they are). The most important problem is that citizens are unable to influence the policies which are implemented, to obtain diversified treatment suited to their own priorities from the bureaucracy, to provide adequate and effective feedback to policy makers, or to avoid demeaning, de-skilling, and de-humanizing treatment from bureaucrats. One of the main problems facing our society is therefore to find ways of making public policy more open, diversified, and responsive. To do this, we will have to develop new ways of providing accountability and variety in the public sector.[3.28]

A large proportion of the problems which remain to be tackled by our society are in the public domain. They have to do with the management of the world economic system and the relationships which are established between national economic systems and the international system—and especially trade between rich and poor countries. They have to do with health services—which need, for example, to establish much more effective community support networks to care for the isolated, the disturbed, the infirm, and the elderly. They have to do with the educational system—which needs to provide much more effective community development networks to promote the growth of competence and, in particular, to promote the development of the civic competencies which are required to operate modern political systems effectively. They have to do with staff placement and development within the public service. They have to do with the quality of the environment, including the built environment. And they have to do with broad ecological issues: pollution control, destruction of the soil, the seas, the air, and the biosphere, and the management of irreplaceable human, physical, and biological resources. They have therefore to do with the very future of our planet, never mind the sustainability of our so-called "civilization" or economy.

This is an appropriate point at which to emphasize that, because activities in all these areas are so central to the quality of life in, and the effectiveness of, modern society, it is necessary to change the way we view them. If public servants are mainly responsible for the quality of our environments, our education, our health; if the agricultural policies they generate have a much greater effect on the amount and quality of food available than anything an individual farmer can do no matter how hard he works, our public servants *create* wealth. Unfortunately these essential, wealth-creating tasks are not being carried out as effectively as they might be—we have, for example, already said that some two thirds of the money spent on "education" is wasted so far as the development of human resources is concerned. It will gradually emerge that, to handle this problem, we need a great deal of fundamental, policy-relevant R&D; to explicitly set out to generate a variety of programs suited to a cross section of the population and information on the personal and social consequences of each—and to feed that information *outward to the public* instead of upward, through a bureaucratic hierarchy, to an assembly of elected representatives. In other words, if our society is to function effectively, we will need new concepts of wealth, wealth-creation, policy evaluation, bureaucracy, and democracy. We will need new tools to administer and evaluate public

30

policy—including the management of the so-called "private" sector ... because that sector is all too prone to foist huge burdens (such as dealing with the pollution and illness it creates) onto the public sector or future generations—and to find ways of holding public servants accountable for acting on information in the public interest.

What these observations imply for the educational system is that it has a major responsibility to nurture the development of the abilities *required to evolve* new civic and economic understandings, the motivation and the capacity to act on insights so gained, and the willingness and the ability to support others who strive to do all of these things.

The Competencies Required in Modern Society: Summary Statement

We may now summarize what we have learned about the qualities required to behave competently in modern society. Competent behavior is, it seems, dependent on:

- The motivation, the beliefs, and the abilities required to engage in high-level, value-laden, activities like taking initiative, exercising responsibility, and analyzing and influencing the operation of organizations and political systems.

- The willingness and the ability to contribute to a climate of support and encouragement for others who are trying to innovate, find better ways of doing things, or take a stand against unethical practices in both the public and private sectors.

- The ability to evolve accurate understandings of how the organization and society in which one lives and works operate and how they are to be influenced—together with appropriate perceptions of one's own role, and that of others, in those organizations.

31

- Appropriate understandings of a number of concepts which relate to the running of organizations. These include such things as risk-taking, efficiency, leadership, responsibility, accountability, communication, equality, participation, wealth and democracy.

The Need for Variety

Having emphasized the need for high-level competencies in all occupational groups and in all walks of life, we must now emphasize both that pupils have the potential to develop a wide variety of very different concerns and talents, and that a wide variety of different patterns of competence are required in society.

Looking first at occupational needs, any occupational group requires a wide range of people who do very different things. Thus Taylor and his colleagues[3.29] have shown that there are 20 different types of outstanding physicians and 12 different types of outstandingly creative scientists. Further, that effective *teams* of scientists, for example, need to be composed of a wide variety of different sorts of people: an ideas man, a fund-raiser, an organizer, a publicist, and so on.

We may generalize these observations. To create the cultures of innovation and development to which the pupils whose views were summarized in Chapter 2 seemed to wish to learn how to contribute, it would be necessary to have a wide variety of people doing very different things: it would be necessary to have some people who were good at organizing others, some who were good at generating better ways of thinking about things, some who were good at finding out how to translate those ideas into effect, some who were good at pouring oil on troubled waters and so on. Put simply: A diversity of high-level talents would be essential.

Reverting to the other side of the coin, we may note that no one person could possibly develop all the concerns and patterns of competence of which we have spoken in this chapter. In fact, we have shown that different pupils want very different things from their education and very different satisfactions from their jobs and their lives. Indeed, there is marked variation in the values and aspirations of pupils who come from similar backgrounds. Most importantly, this variation is related to the occupational destinations for which they are bound. There is also a great deal more inter-generational social mobility—both upward and downward—than many people would have us believe. Payne[3.30] showed that 72% of adults in Scotland had been upwardly or downwardly mobile by at least 1 category, and 20% of those who held the highest positions had come from the very lowest group. Hope[3.31] has shown that the same is true of the United States. The maintenance of our social structure is therefore a great deal more complex than many have suggested. The evidence therefore points very strongly toward the need to respect and build on the variance in pupils' values, priorities, and patterns of competence (instead of trying to inculcate middle-class values into working-class children). The specter of teachers perpetuating socio-economic divisions, reproducing the social order, and creating a caste society if they respect the variation in pupils' values, concerns, and talents therefore seems to be ill-founded.[3.32]

Summary

Pupils, parents, teachers, and employers are correct: a wide variety of high-level competencies is required for the effective operation of modern society. Unexpectedly, these talents consist of value-laden motivational dispositions which are centrally dependent on beliefs about how society works and one's own role within it. Fears of teachers perpetuating the social order if they respected, and sought to nurture, the diversity of pupils' concerns and talents, are probably exaggerated.

CHAPTER 4

THE NATURE OF COMPETENCE

In this chapter, the nature of competence will be illuminated by analyzing "initiative" as one example of a high-level competence. However, it would have been possible to present an exactly parallel analysis of "problem solving ability," "the ability to communicate," or any other high-level competence.

Self Motivated

The first feature of initiative to which attention should be drawn is that it is a *self-motivated* quality. It does not make sense to record as evidence of 'initiative' any behavior which someone else has told the individual concerned to carry out. The significance of this observation is that, if we wish to nurture such qualities as "initiative," "the ability to identify and solve problems" or "the ability to communicate," we will have to teach our children, pupils, or trainees to *trigger the relevant behaviors for themselves*. In other words, we will not only have to foster sensitivity to the cues—often dim feelings of attraction or repulsion in various parts of the body—which tell them when such behaviors are appropriate, we will also have to create opportunities for them to experience the satisfactions which come from having undertaken such activities effectively—for it is the repeated experience of such satisfactions that will lead them to engage in these activities in the future.

Demanding and Internally Heterogeneous

Next, it should be noted that, if people are to take a successful initiative, they will have to devote a great deal of time, thought, and effort to the activity: they will have to initiate potentially innovative action (often on the basis of hunches or feelings), "monitor" the effects of that action (again often relying on the feelings which usually precede new insights), and learn from those effects more about the nature of the problem they are trying to tackle and the effectiveness of the strategies they are using. They will have to persist over long periods of time. They will have to wake up at night in an effort to seize on flickering glimmerings of understanding on the fringe of consciousness and bring them to the center of attention so that they become fully conscious and usable. They will have to pry information out of other people's heads—often information which those concerned do not know they have or which they are unwilling to share. They will have to anticipate obstacles in the future and invent ways of circumventing them. They will have to persuade other people to help. They will have to build up their own, unique, set of *specialist* knowledge of the nature of the problem, its causes, and potential solutions. The latter will often involve building up an understanding of how the organization in which they live or work functions and identifying "leverage" points at which it can be influenced.

The same applies to competencies like the ability to identify and solve problems or communicate effectively. To identify a problem, one has to become dimly aware of feelings that tell one that something is wrong or which point toward a potential solution. (Note that these feelings form *part* of the ability to cognize). One has to persist in the face of frustration and difficulty. (Note that this, too, forms part of the ability to cognize). One has to persuade others to help. One has to initiate "experimental (often feeling-based) interactions with the environment" to test one's emerging, feeling-based "hypotheses." And so on. All of these form part of the ability to make one's own observations. And all are difficult and demanding activities which are heavily dependent on "unconscious" processes which have time spans of their own and cannot be accessed on request.

The same applies to the ability to communicate. This involves clarifying what it is that one wants to convey and how to convey it—often without saying it. It involves experimenting with different forms of communication such as gesture, innuendo, allusion, and using images to conjure up feelings which in turn convey ideas and understandings which have never been expressed in words, and being sensitive to one's feelings in order to monitor the reactions of one's audience.

Qualities like adventurousness require many of the competencies mentioned above plus others, like sensitivity to the cues which tell one when things are getting dangerous and out of hand and that one had either better stop or get help; sensitivity to the cues which tell one how far one can let a situation go before it becomes non-recoverable, experience of recovering situations which are on the verge of getting out of hand, the kind of sensitivity which leads one to notice things which one had not set out to look for but which represent new discoveries, and the abilities required to capitalize on new observations once they have been made.

Value-based

No one is going to do any of these things unless they care very much indeed about the activity in the course of which they are attempting to take initiative, solve problems, communicate, or whatever.

It follows from these observations that the kinds of activity which people value are central to competence and thus to fostering and assessing its components. People cannot be expected to develop important components of competence unless they practice them in the course of undertaking activities which they care about. Likewise, it does not make sense to attempt to assess such competencies except while those concerned are doing things they do care about. Unless they are doing things they value, people's failure to display high-level competencies simply reveals that they, personally, do not care about the task they were asked to undertake (however much they may value some external benefit which effective performance of the task might bring).

36

Interpenetrating Cognitive, Affective and Conative Components

Another insight to be drawn out of this analysis is that high-level competencies involve extensive use of feelings and demand determination and persistence. What have been termed their cognitive, affective, and conative components therefore interpenetrate.

Cumulative and Substitutable Components

Yet another conclusion which needs to be noted is that activities are more likely to be successful if the person concerned is able to perform *many* of the component activities mentioned above. Thus components of competence are cumulative and substitutable. It follows that high-level competencies are not internally consistent in the psychometric or factorial sense: it is the *total number* of the independent and substitutable components of competence which an individual displays in pursuit of his or her valued goals that relates to success. Models of human abilities which either emphasize internal consistency or focus only on cognitions are therefore seriously off-target.

Numerous Possibly Valued Activities and Components of Competence

One last thing we should note is that there appears to be an almost endless array of activities which people may value and competencies which may be brought to bear to undertake any one of those activities effectively. One of the things we most urgently need is, therefore, a taxonomy—like the taxonomy of chemical elements—which will enable us to organize the domain into which we have stumbled, show which values and competencies relate to which other ones, and enable us to analyze more complex qualities into their elements. A preliminary attempt to provide such a framework has been published in *Competence in Modern Society*, but a great deal of further work is needed.

37

Other Components of Competence

Table 4.1 presents some other qualities, or components of competence, which schools might try to foster. These competencies are not listed in any order and the list is incomplete. The list is simply included as a basis for discussion.

It is useful to examine what might be meant by "self-confidence"—and how "it" might be fostered in slightly more detail because so many people have argued that it is important for schools to foster it.

One type of confidence is confidence that one can make one's own observations, find information for oneself, and learn *without* instruction. If one is to do these things, one has to be confident that one can identify the vague feelings which tell one that one has a problem or the germ of its solution and bring them

---

TABLE 4.1
Some Components of Competence.

- Confidence that one can engage in a number of the following types of competent behavior.
- Tendency to notice *problems* which will interfere with goal attainment.
- Tendency to notice resources which can lead to establishment of goals, or to their attainment.
- Ability to lead effectively—the ability to articulate group goals and unleash the energies of others in pursuit of them.
- Ability to follow effectively—the spontaneous tendency to study and seek to understand an overall program of activity—and one's own place in it—without having to be given detailed instructions.
- Tendency to engage in integrated thought-action-feedback strategies.
- Willingness to tolerate the anxieties which swell up in the course of achieving new and important goals.
- The tendency to bring to bear the relevant past experiences.
- Ability to integrate complex information in a subjective manner rather than to focus on one or two inadequate criteria.
- Sensitivity to one's own feelings and emotions and willingness to unleash them in the service of goal attainment.
- Tendency to make standards explicit.
- Ability to set up win-win relationships with others to achieve joint goals.

---

up into full consciousness. To be willing to do this, one has not only to have had practice at doing it, one has also to have had sufficient experience of doing it to have learned that engaging in such frustrating and time-consuming activities tends to be worthwhile and to pay off in the end. Then one has to mull over the implications of one's observations, and initiate courses of action which will enable one to find out if one's tentative understandings are correct. One has to have learned that one does not solve one's problems *simply* by sitting and thinking about them. One has to have learned that one learns a great deal from interacting with one's environment and monitoring the effects of one's actions. This means initiating "experimental interaction with one's environment" on the basis of hunches or feelings and attending to the feelings evoked by what happens to learn more about the situation one is dealing with and the effectiveness of one's strategies. In other words, to develop confidence that one can learn on one's own, *without* instruction, one has to have had experience of successfully undertaking all the activities mentioned above in the course of doing things one cares about.

Another type of self-confidence involves confidence that one can get other people to help one. This in turn involves confidence that one can persuade other people, perhaps using gesture, innuendo, and imagery to create in others the kinds of feelings that compel action. It involves having had experience of playing a leadership role which involves clarifying group goals and convincing other people that, through joint action, they can be achieved. It involves confidence that one can express oneself adequately. It involves confidence that other people will not regard one as the sort of person to whom they should not listen. It involves the ability to be sensitive to the worries which other people have, but have not clearly articulated, let alone expressed. This in turn implies sensitivity to slight feelings on the edge of one's own consciousness. Sensitivity to others therefore depends on sensitivity to oneself. It follows that developing this type of self-confidence involves having had ample experience of engaging in these high-level cognitive, affective, and goal-directed activities. And it implies having engaged in them in an integrated manner in relation to goals which are important to one.

Yet another type of self-confidence is confidence in one's ability to contribute to a team. This involves being able to identify the type of contribution one is best able to make—something which implies having had opportunities to contribute in different ways to a group process and acquaintance with the concepts which are required to think about the nature of the contribution one has made and compare and contrast it with the type of contribution made by others. It involves being able to persuade others to listen and to play their part and recognize one's own contribution.

Implications for Education and Assessment

Each of the other qualities listed in the table could also be discussed at similar length. However enough has been said to underline the following points made in our earlier discussion of initiative:

(1) It is impossible to foster the qualities identified in the previous chapters except in relation to goals that pupils care about.

(2) All of the qualities which it is important to foster are value-laden **motivational dispositions** which—even at the "lowest" level—involve beliefs about society, how it works, and one's own role in it.

(3) Because it is important to foster motivation, it is necessary to both help pupils to identify their incipient motives and concerns and ensure that they have opportunities to experience the satisfactions which come from engaging in the difficult and demanding activities which are required to undertake valued activities effectively.

(4) There are so many potentially important components of competence that no pupil can be expected to develop all of them. Some pupils will have the inclination and the ability to develop one selection of them while others will have the inclination, the interests, and the talents that are required to develop a quite different set of qualities.[4.1]

(5) Just as these qualities cannot be fostered except in relation to goals which pupils value, so neither can they be assessed except in relation to those goals. This points to the need for a two-stage measurement model in which we first find out what people care about and then ask how many—and which—high-level competencies they display while undertaking those tasks. A psychometric model which takes account of these observations has been published in *Competence in Modern Society: Its Identification, Development and Release* and, in summary form (but accompanied by a discussion of the destructive effects of the forms of assessment that are most widely used at the present time), in Trillium Press's companion volume: *The Tragic Illusion: Educational Testing*.[4.2]

CHAPTER 5

SCHOOLS NEGLECT THEIR MAIN GOALS; WORSE: THEY ARE SOCIALLY DYSFUNCTIONAL

So far, we have seen that it is widely agreed that the main goals of education include fostering high-level competencies like initiative, the ability to communicate, and the ability and willingness to seek to understand and influence the way society works. We have seen that these opinions are correct. And we have learned enough about the psychological nature of such qualities to have a feel for the type of educational activity which is likely to be necessary if they are to be nurtured.

The next question is: how effectively do schools achieve these, their most important, goals?

Tables 5.1 and 5.2 give the percentages of teachers who said they tried "very hard" to achieve each objective with "more academic" pupils and the proportion who felt that schools were "very" or "moderately" successful in achieving each objective. (It was necessary to combine "very" and "moderately successful" categories in order to obtain even the relatively low levels of perceived success shown here).

The first thing to note is that "getting pupils through examinations"—which came 23rd in the teachers' "importance" ranking—has jumped into first position in terms of the attention it actually gets. It seems that pupils' and parents' desire for credentials, combined with teachers' need to be esteemed good teachers by this criterion, has markedly affected their behavior. Helping their pupils to get high achievement test scores is also the only objective which significantly more than half of them thought the educational system achieved even moderately well.

The other items at the top of teachers' rated behavioral priorities have to do with ensuring that pupils treat each other

TABLE 5.1

Objectives Receiving Most Attention.

Percentage of Teachers (other than Heads) who Tried Very Hard to Achieve Each Objective in Their Own Lessons With the "More Academic" Pupils.

	%
1. Help them to do as well as possible in external examinations like the Intermediate, Group or Leaving Certificates	78
2. Help them to develop a considerate attitude towards other people.	63
3. Make sure that they really enjoy the lesson.	61
4. Encourage them to have opinions of their own.	60
5. Encourage them to have a sense of duty towards the community.	59
6. Make sure that they are able to read and study on their own.	59
7. Teach them about what is right and wrong.	57
8. Ensure that all students can express themselves clearly in writing.	57
9. Ensure that all pupils can speak well and put what they want to say into words easily.	55
10. Encourage pupils to be independent and to be able to stand on their own feet.	53
11. Help them to develop their characters and personalities.	53
12. Ensure that they are aware of aspects of your subject which they do not have to know for the examinations.	49
13. Help them to get on with other people.	46
14. Make sure that they get an education that is so interesting, useful and enjoyable that they will be keen to continue their formal education in adult life.	45
15. Give them experience of taking responsibility.	44
16. Ensure that they know how to apply the facts and techniques they have learned to new problems.	39
17. Make sure they get a thorough religious education.	38
18. Help them to take an interest in and to understand what is going on in the world now.	37
19. Ensure that they can formulate hypotheses, seek evidence and reason logically.	37
20. Make sure they are confident and at ease in dealing with people.	36
21. To make sure they go out in the world determined to make Ireland a better place in which to live.	34
22. Help them to think out what they really want to achieve in life.	34
23. To ensure that they leave school confident, willing and able to take the initiative in introducing changes.	31
24. Ensure that all pupils feel at home with figures and numbers.	29
25. Tell them about different sorts of jobs and careers so that they can decide what they want to do.	27
26. Teach them things that will be of direct use to them when they start work in their jobs or careers.	27
27. Ensure that they leave school intent on being masters of their own destinies.	26
28. Enable them to develop an interest in subjects other than those studied for examinations.	26
29. Give them information about the courses of Further and Higher Education that are open to them.	25
30. Ensure that they are aware of the prolonged struggle for Irish freedom and are determined to uphold the ideals which inspired it.	22
31. Run clubs and societies (e.g. sports, hobbies, social and youth clubs) for pupils out of school hours.	19
32. Teach them about a wide range of cultures and philosophies so that their own can be seen to be one of many.	16
33. Help them to understand the implications and responsibilities of marriage.	14
34. Advise parents to give sex education to their children.	10
35. Provide the pupils with sex education in the school.	10
36. Teach them about bringing up children, home repairs, decorating and so on.	10
37. Teach them to be sceptical, that is to take little on trust.	10
38. Encourage them to have a good time.	7
39. Introduce them to new subjects e.g. philosophy, sociology, archaeology etc.	5

Weighted base (= 100%) all teachers other than heads rating objectives for "more academic" pupils: 528.

TABLE 5.2

Success with which Educational Objectives are Attained.

Percentage of Teachers Saying Education "Very Successful" or "Moderately Successful" in Achieving Each Objective with the "More Academic" Pupils.

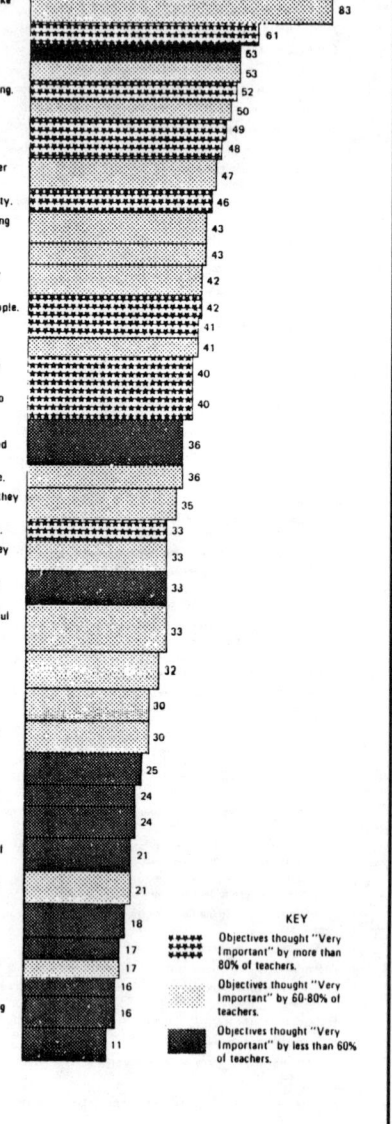

1. Help them to do as well as possible in external examinations like the Intermediate, Group or Leaving Certificates. — 83
2. Teach them about what is right and wrong. — 61
3. Ensure that all pupils feel at home with figures and numbers. — 53
4. Make sure they get a thorough religious education. — 53
5. Ensure that all students can express themselves clearly in writing. — 52
6. Help them to get on with other people. — 50
7. Help them to develop their characters and personalities. — 49
8. Encourage them to have opinions of their own. — 48
9. Give them information about the courses of Further and Higher Education that are open to them. — 47
10. Encourage them to have a sense of duty towards the community. — 46
11. Help them to take an interest in and to understand what is going on in the world now. — 43
12. Give them experience of taking responsibility. — 43
13. Tell them about different sorts of jobs and careers so that they can decide what they want to do. — 42
14. Help them to develop a considerate attitude towards other people. — 42
15. Make sure that they are able to read and study on their own. — 41
16. Make sure that they really enjoy the lesson. — 41
17. Encourage pupils to be independent and to be able to stand on their own feet. — 40
18. Ensure that all pupils can speak well and put what they want to say into words easily. — 40
19. Ensure that they are aware of the prolonged struggle for Irish freedom and are determined to uphold the ideals which inspired it. — 36
20. Make sure they are confident and at ease in dealing with people. — 36
21. Ensure that they know how to apply the facts and techniques they have learned to new problems. — 35
22. Help them to think out what they really want to achieve in life. — 33
23. Ensure that they are aware of aspects of your subject which they do not have to know for the examinations. — 33
24. Teach them things that will be of direct use to them when they start work in their jobs or careers. — 33
25. Make sure that they get an education that is so interesting, useful and enjoyable that they will be keen to continue their formal education in adult life. — 33
26. To ensure that they leave school confident, willing and able to take the initiative in introducing changes. — 32
27. Ensure that they can formulate hypotheses, seek evidence and reason logically. — 30
28. To make sure they go out in the world determined to make Ireland a better place in which to live. — 30
29. Run clubs and societies (e.g. sports, hobbies, social and youth clubs) for pupils out of school hours. — 25
30. Provide the pupils with sex education in the school. — 24
31. Ensure that they leave school intent on being masters of their destinies. — 24
32. Help them to understand the implications and responsibilities of marriage. — 21
33. Enable them to develop an interest in subjects other than those studied for examinations. — 21
34. Teach them about a wide range of cultures and philosophies so that their own can be seen to be one of many. — 18
35. Teach them to be sceptical, that is to take little on trust. — 17
36. Advise parents to give sex education to their children. — 17
37. Encourage them to have a good time. — 16
38. Teach them about bringing up children, home repairs, decorating and so on. — 16
39. Introduce them to new subjects e.g. philosophy, sociology, archaeology etc. — 11

KEY

★★★★★ Objectives thought "Very Important" by more than 80% of teachers.

Objectives thought "Very Important" by 60-80% of teachers.

■■■ Objectives thought "Very Important" by less than 60% of teachers.

Weighted base (100%)

All teachers answering for the "more academic" pupils. 612.

with a minimum of respect and do not disrupt each other's work. It seems that the need to do these basic things—perhaps even to socialize their pupils—has forced teachers to spend time doing things which did not figure among their top *educational* priorities. They even feel that they have to entertain their pupils instead of educating them.

These verbal reports by teachers on what they devote their time to have been confirmed by classroom observation studies conducted on both sides of the Atlantic.[5.1]

In the course of his vast study of 8,624 parents, 1,350 teachers, 17,163 students, and 1,000 classrooms, Goodlad,[5.2] like Flanagan[5.3] and Johnston[5.4] before him, found that American elementary and high school students spend most of their time in boring, non-cumulative, routine activities—largely being talked at in classes on language, spelling, and arithmetic. Drill and practice predominate. The "academic" and "intellectual" activities which are undertaken barely deserve the name: they rarely involve analyzing, evaluating, hypothesizing, interpreting, judging, reconciling different points of view, or re-conceptualizing problems, let alone identifying and understanding new problems. There is little enquiry-oriented activity, still less sensitive, respectful facilitation of the development of students' particular talents. "Teachers did not respond to students because students rarely initiated anything." There is little opportunity for students to practice doing such things as thinking, planning, inventing, communicating, reassuring, leading, working with others, or developing their own understanding of how society works and taking the initiative to influence it. They are therefore unable to experience the satisfactions which come from doing these things, develop the motivation to do them, or develop the abilities required to do them successfully.

Instead of being expected to develop self-direction and self-discipline, pupils are generally goaded to work. They get little help with their problems.

Little is done to capitalize on potential sources of motivation—to, for example, encourage students to develop communication skills by first ensuring that they have something that they **want** to communicate, and are therefore in a frame of mind to seek feed-back. Instead, most of the time is devoted to communicating teacher-generated "rules" for "effective communication," and to such things as students underlining verbs and adverbs in sentences in the belief that this will lead them to write "correctly."

Traditional frontal teaching predominates. Few teachers succeed in catering for the wide variety of talents and abilities which are present in every classroom. Nor do they vary their teaching methods or the content they teach so as to engage the attention of all of the students for at least some of the time.[5.5]

These results have been confirmed in virtually every detail by research carried out in England and Scotland.[5.6]

The IEA Civics study[5.7] enquired whether teachers made use of the educational methods which would have been likely to lead to the development of the competencies, understandings, and knowledge which would be required to exercise different forms of citizenship. Few were doing so. Indeed few even understood the objectives or nature of the curriculum processes which would have enabled them to foster any of the forms of civic competence identified by the authors of the study.

It will, of course, be claimed that schools have changed since these data were collected. Certainly numerous papers have been generated and endless administrators' and teachers' time has, as in the past, been devoted to talking about change. But there are a number of reasons for remaining skeptical about the actual impact. My previous experience[5.8] suggests that talk is (relatively) cheap and that it is very difficult to introduce significant change. Secondly, the barriers to change that have been identified in the course of our work (see Chapter 7) are so deep-rooted that it is extremely difficult to believe that there has been much change behind classroom doors. Thirdly, colleagues who are actively engaged in schools—whether as researchers or as school psychologists—as well as my own children and their friends—tell me that little has happened on the ground. Fourthly, there are a number of publications[5.9] which confirm the impression. It would therefore seem that, until firm evidence to the contrary is produced, we must assume that schools remain much as they were when the research summarized above was carried out—which also means that they are much as they were when we were at school.

Students' Reactions to their Education

In Goodlad's study, only English and Mathematics were considered **important** by more than two-thirds of high school students—and that for the future, not the present. Unfortunately, students will forget much of what they have been taught within two years, so even their hope that their studies will one day be of value to them is ill-founded. School subjects are boring: only Arts, P.E., and Languages were rated as interesting by more than one-third of those taking them. These results again correspond to the results of studies which have been carried out in the UK,[5.10] Belgium,[5.11] Ireland[5.12] and Scotland.[5.13] More than half of the adolescents interviewed rated more than half of their subjects **both** boring and useless. More than half wanted schools to do more to achieve more than 90% of the objectives we asked them about. Bill et al[5.14] found that 98% of a random sample of high school students felt they were failures at school.

It would seem to follow from these results that the climates which characterize school classrooms cannot be conducive to well-being and development. Still less can the students be getting opportunities to practice and develop the patterns of thought and behavior which we all associate with adventurous, enterprising, innovative activity. Nor can they be being offered opportunities to engage in the kinds of individualized, self-motivated, activities which would be required if they are to undertake activities they care about and in the process develop a range of high-level competencies.

The explanation of pupils' bleak comments cannot be that young people have unduly high expectations or are negativistic. What they say about their schools compares very unfavorably with what their older peers say about work and with what they themselves will say about it a few years later. In our surveys, 80% of ex-pupils who had left school at the first opportunity said—after they had been at work for five years, and in response to three separate questions—that they liked their jobs, liked their employers, and found their jobs interesting. This was largely because—in contrast to the circumstances which prevailed at school—they were able to move themselves into positions in which they were able to do things they liked doing and were good at instead of being forced to do many things they did not like and were not good at. But it was also because they were able to take initiative and because making the most of themselves was appreciated. Grannis,[5.15] Bachman,[5.16] Flanagan[5.17] and Robinson[5.18] obtained similar results in the United States. It is not, of course, true that all jobs are so satisfying. But even in the "worst" jobs—jobs in large manufacturing plants and large offices such as insurance companies—the levels of satisfaction only fell to around 60% ... still much higher than those obtained from pupils while at school.

It emerges, therefore, that school work is actually the worst and least developmental work in our society ... and that school environments are the least conducive to feelings of well-being. (Of course, this does not show they are socially dysfunctional at least in the short term: Marxists have long maintained that one of the functions of schools is to lead students to tolerate otherwise intolerable working conditions.)

Ex-pupils' Reactions

Bachman et al[5.19] found that whereas only 13% of adolescents at school said they had had opportunities to identify and develop their talents, the proportion of young adults who said they had been able to do this at work was 80%. Leona Tyler,[5.20] commenting (with Gagne, Scriven, Ralph Tyler and others) on the implications of what Flanagan's respondents—the Project Talent Sample—had, at 30 years of age, to say about the connection between education and work, noted that the most logical conclusion was that schools should be closed down. (She, of course, recognized that this could not be done since the main function of schools is the sociological one of keeping young adults out of the labour market). Most of the employed adults we interviewed said that at school they had not learned things which were useful in their jobs or in their leisure.[5.21] Although a significant proportion of those in middle class occupations said that their education had helped them to get a good job, working class people did not even derive this benefit from their education.

In two of our own studies,[5.22] and in Flanagan's[5.23] study, ex-pupils were asked to identify the benefits they had derived from their education. Only a small proportion were able to report any benefits—but those they did report involved the development of qualities like those which came at the top of the pupils' list of priorities as reported in Chapter 2. Where these qualities had been developed, it was chiefly while they held positions of responsibility as prefects or in clubs and societies. A similar conclusion emerges from the work of Collins[5.24] and that of the Centre for Educational Sociology in Edinburgh.[5.25]

Teachers' Knowledge of Pupils' Values

The observation that most schools cannot be doing much to foster high-level competencies is supported by the following observations.

As we have seen, if teachers are to foster high-level competencies, they need to create activities which build on the pupils' values. But the available data[5.26] show that many teachers hardly know their pupils—still less their values: indeed they (like Goodlad[5.27]) systematically underestimate their pupils' serious mindedness. Most teachers feel obliged to pressurize their pupils, in an autocratic manner, to work toward attainment tests in which they themselves do not believe and which they think confer few benefits on their pupils. This tendency is exacerbated by the fact that they know that many of their pupils are bored and disinterested, and they believe that the pupils themselves do not wish to acquire the credentials. They therefore cannot trust their pupils to work on their own or set about creating developmental environments in which pupils would individually be encouraged to do things they cared about. They are therefore in no position to find out what their pupils' individual interests and values are, let alone work toward different goals with different pupils. Unfortunately, we have seen that, if the main goals of education are to be achieved, educational programs must be individualized so that pupils can do things they care about.

It is not only the certification system which prevents teachers from getting to know and respect their pupils. When teachers were asked to say what the main goals of education should be for different groups of pupils, it emerged that they thought that the same goals *should* be pursued by *all* pupils.[5.28] Not only were the same goals appropriate for all, they themselves felt that they were at the time of the study offering courses directed toward the same goals for all pupils—indeed that the goals were equally well (or, more correctly, equally badly) achieved by all pupils. Once again, one may ask: how could schools possibly be effectively nurturing individual talents in such a climate?

Finally, although, as we have seen, if high-level competencies are to be fostered, it is necessary for different pupils to do different things, two-thirds of the teachers we interviewed defined less academic pupils as "less intelligent, less able, and no good at anything." Only one-third described them as pupils with other abilities. This single-factor model of the intellect is inimical to diversified provision and, once again, supports the conclusion that schools *cannot* be reaching the—widely agreed—manifest goals of education.

More Direct Evidence that Schools are not Achieving their Wider Goals

So far, we have suggested that schools cannot be achieving their main goals very effectively because classroom environments are not conducive to the exercise and development of high-level competencies, because teachers do not know, and are rarely in a position to find out, what their pupils' values are, and be-

50

cause many teachers are unable, and often unwilling, to individualize provision. While convincing, this evidence is necessarily indirect. We have made two attempts to collect more direct evidence about whether high-level competencies are developed. One of these was the IEA 'Civics' study.[5.29] This showed that most pupils had not developed initiative, the ability to work with others, respect for people with other values and talents, or a willingness to play an active part in society.

The other study involved a more general evaluation of primary school classrooms.[5.30] One finding was that the role models to whom most pupils were exposed in their teachers were unlikely to be conducive to the development of self-confidence, adventurousness, and initiative. Teachers emerged as the most down-trodden, lacking in self-confidence, and least confident of their ability to gain control of their destinies of any of the occupational groups we studied. It is difficult to see how people who lack self-confidence—and particularly confidence in their ability to manage self-starting others—are going to be able to nurture self-confidence in others. A second observation was that the classroom processes present in most classrooms were unlikely to lead to the development of high-level qualities. A third finding, derived from a study of what pupils in different types of classrooms thought the consequences would be if they were to try to do something about problems they cared about, was that pupils in most classrooms felt that they would not know where to begin any attempt to tackle the problems and that the exercise would end up being a disastrous mess. (In the next chapter we will summarize the results of our studies of the more effective of these classrooms.)

The Value of Present School Activities

So far, we have seen that schools neither attend to, nor achieve, their main goals. But is what they do teach of much value?

Clearly, what schools teach is of great use to some pupils because, as a result of passing examinations, they are able to enter protected occupations which afford security and success-fully deter competitors. However, as we have seen, pupils discriminate sharply between the importance they attach to obtaining grades or credentials and the importance they attach to the *content* of their studies. It is the latter we are concerned with here.

On *a priori* grounds it seems unlikely that schooling can be of great intrinsic value. Once they move beyond the "3Rs," schools focus on conveying *knowledge* to their pupils instead of fostering competencies. Unfortunately, knowledge has a half-life of one year. Thus, pupils forget 50% of what they have been taught after one year, 75% after two years, $87^1/_2$% after three years and so on. Furthermore, as is well known, most of the information taught to pupils in schools is already ten or more years out of date. It rarely matches the pupils' needs: the knowledge explosion means that the probability that pupils will at school be introduced to a significant amount of the knowledge they will later require is extremely small. There is so much to select from and much of what they will actually need to know does not yet exist. This means that the chances of them actually requiring much of what they have to "master" to obtain high grades is extremely small. To do their jobs well they will require unique combinations of up-to-date specialist knowledge, not what they have retained of the smatterings of low-level, out of date, bodies of knowledge that are often referred to as "disciplines."

As has already been reported, a study we conducted in Edin-burgh, Scotland showed that most adults do not think that their education has been very useful at work, in their lives outside work, or even in getting a job. However, about half of the middle

52

class group did feel that their education had been useful in obtaining a job, but rather fewer felt it had been useful in their jobs.

Schools' failure to confer many useful benefits on their students is more fully documented in the studies reported by Berg,[5.31] Jencks *et al,*[5.32] Flanagan,[5.33] Bachman *et al*[5.34] and Collins.[5.35] If—and Flanagan's[5.36] and Schon's[5.37] data show that it is a big if—academic knowledge is required in later life it is either necessary to find it for oneself or to take specialist courses.

Do Schools Do Actual Harm?

Many authors (eg, Reimer,[5.38] Holt,[5.39] Goodman,[5.40] Freire[5.41]) have asserted that schools *stunt* the growth of competence. Few careful studies exist, but those that do (eg, Winter and McClelland,[5.42] Freedman and Berg,[5.43] Bill *et al,*[5.44] Collins,[5.45] Raven[5.46]) generally support the thesis. Pupils develop feelings of *in*competence, trained incapacity, and failure. They come to call for courses and information instead of developing the competencies and the confidence required to forge and find their own information. They learn to call on someone else to tackle their problems.

There are actually two distinct ways in which schools do harm. On the one hand, they stunt the growth of the pupils and instill dysfunctional beliefs and attitudes. On the other, they select and promote a disproportionate number of the wrong people into influential positions in society. The second of these may be part of a wider process whereby, as we will see in Chapter 7, the educational system appears to operate as fraudulently as the marketplace itself and functions in such a way as to create jobs and the kind of discriminations which act to compel participation in both education and the marketplace. It also operates in such a way as to result in laying the blame for the ills of society at the door of the disadvantaged and those who are compelled to fail at school (and who are thus in no position to do anything about the problems of society) rather than at the door of those who do well in the system and who therefore end up in the positions from which they are best placed to do something about the problems. While these processes are (at least in the longer term) socially dysfunctional, they are primarily sociological rather than educational. For this reason, and because these processes mainly operate to drive any form of multiple-talent education out of schools (because these would fail to produce the kinds of discriminations which are required to compel participation in the educational system and the institutions of modern society), these topics will not be discussed here.

Willis[5.47] demonstrated that some pupils reacted to the demeaning environments provided by schools by learning how to analyze and see through middle-class rhetoric, how to appease authority, how to give the impression of working while not in fact doing so, and how to maintain a supportive peer group and thus preserve their self-respect. He concluded that schools teach at least some pupils how to cope with the workplace; that is, how to "labor" in ways which were personally functional in the conditions which prevail in many workplaces—although perhaps not achieving the goals of employers. Somewhat oddly, however, he failed to note that schools may teach very many more pupils to labor in exactly those ways that are required in many "white collar" occupations. Thus he failed to note that, as Tomlinson and Tenhouten[5.48] observed, pupils can not only be expected to learn, but actually do learn, how to secure their own advancement by working out what those above them want to hear and then saying whatever is necessary to secure their preferment *without* doing the work which is ostensibly necessary for that advancement.

Although the development of this competence should be highly functional from the point of view of the individuals concerned, given the environmental, financial, and organizational crises facing our society, the promotion of pupils with such preoccupations and skills into influential positions could (and Hope[5.49] has observed that it actually is) be highly dysfunctional from the point of view of society. Although, in the short term, people with such concerns seem to be ideally suited to manning the fraudulent[5.50] organizations of which our society is so largely composed, in the longer term, double talk and the substitution of high-sounding words and inappropriate action (based, for example, on social and economic theories which do not withstand any careful scrutiny) for public-spirited action to tackle the crucial problems which face us, cannot be other than disastrous.

With these reflections in mind, it is interesting to reconsider Bernstein's[5.51] claim that the substitution of "multiple and implicit" goals for the traditional "3Rs" in elementary schools—ostensibly designed to enable more pupils to develop more of their talents—may be more correctly viewed as creating conditions in which some pupils can be trained to work out for themselves what to do to obtain preferment in a situation of limited opportunities and then get on and do it.

Is the Social Allotment Performed by Schools Functional?

Whether we like it or not, schools **do** allocate pupils' future occupational position and status. The extent of the relationship in Ireland is illustrated in the following table. Jencks suggests that the relationship is not so striking in America. However, Hope[5.52] has shown that, by age 40, the association between IQ (for which years of education is a surrogate) and social mobility—both upward and downward—is the same in the USA and Scotland (and Ireland may be much the same). The question we now have to consider is the extent to which the social allocative role performed by schools is functional and dysfunctional—bearing in mind that what is functional for the individual may be dysfunctional for society.

TABLE 5.3
Relate Sexual Status of Persons Completing Secondary School but then Terminating Their Education.

	Son's status (%)		
Father's status	Higher	Same	Lower
1. Professional and high administration	—	28	72
2. Inspectional, supervisory, etc.	13	23	57
3. Skilled manual, routine non-manual	52	36	12
4. Unskilled	94	6	—
*From Hutchinson, B. (1969).			

Although it is widely believed that the social placement functions which schools perform for society, while not desirable, at least result in the "more able" pupils being selected for influential positions in society, that assumption has been questioned by such authors as Berg,[5.53] Goodman,[5.54] Tomlinson and Tenhouten,[5.55] Nuttgens,[5.56] Bernstein,[5.57] Dore[5.58] and even by Hope[5.59] (after he had demonstrated that 60% of social mobility can be explained by IQ). More generally, one whole strand of the Progressive Education movement has been based on some teachers' observation that the kinds of pupils that are favoured by the educational system are not those who possess the talents and concerns which are required to contribute to society.

Given Hope's data on the relationship between IQ and occupational status finally attained, the answer to the question obviously depends on what one means by "more able." Hope's challenge is very obviously based on querying whether the *values* of those whom the educational system selects for, and places in, influential positions are appropriate. The same question lies behind the challenges of several of the other authors mentioned, including the "anti-academic" wing of the Progressive Education movement.

In the course of our own work we were able to analyze adolescents' educational values, work values, and family and social values by both their social origins and the socio-economic status—indeed the detailed occupational categories—of the jobs they expected to enter. What we found was that many of the attitudes and values which are known to be associated with socio-economic status were more closely related to where pupils were *going to* than where they came from. Thus, we found that pupils who expected to enter high status jobs were much more concerned than others to develop independence, the abilities required to make their own observations, and those required to take responsibility. Pupils bound for low status positions, whatever their origins, were more concerned than others to be given strict rules to guide their lives and were much less keen to develop originality, independence, or initiative. Instead, these pupils stressed obedience, sex education, religious education and developing toughness and strength. Thus, it would seem that Kohn's[5.60] original (and widely cited) claim that such values and attitudes are acquired as a result of experience in different occupational roles is open to question—as, indeed, Kohn himself now recognizes. People seem to be sorted according to their attitudes and beliefs in such a way that they end up in occupational groups which possess similar concerns and attitudes. Kinsey[5.61] had much earlier noted the same thing in relation to sexual beliefs and attitudes—and in this case, there is little possibility of adolescents having learned the relevant attitudes and behaviors through explicit tuition or by observation. More recently, Bouchard,[5.62] Lykken[5.63] and others have shown from twin studies that experience in the home contributes very little to the documented variance in personality and attitudes—including religious beliefs.

So far, so good. Although the results lead us to question the desirability of enrichment programs in which pupils from all backgrounds are encouraged to strive to do well in the school system, they do appear to suggest that the allocative process is functional. However, the picture is not quite so simple. The highly upwardly mobile pupils in our survey were much more anxious than anyone else to obtain high test scores and to cut out the "frills" of education—such as developing the ability to work with others, the desire to work for the good of the community, and initiative. Promotion of such self-interested individuals into high status positions could be extremely damaging for the organizations in which they will work and the society in which they will live. That this is more than a mere possibility is confirmed in our studies of employees in a wide variety of organizations. There, we found, as did Berg,[5.64] that such ambitious individuals tended to do such things as get rid of the time and the arrangements that Kanter[5.65] has shown are essential to future development and innovation—ie, they vandalized those workplaces—for the sake of short term "efficiency" and their personal promotion prospects.

57

A final—and, from the point of view of examining the functional significance of the social allocative processes currently operating in society, very important—finding from our survey was that those who were *most* anxious to work for the long term good of society and the communities in which they lived were those who both came from, and were bound for, high status positions. Background socialization *does* play a role and it may be important to build some of the relevant experiences into educational programs.

In summing up our own work, it is fair to say that, not only does our IEA data[5.66] show that pupils at school have developed some highly dysfunctional overall attitudes, expectations, and values, the social placement functions performed by the educational system currently operate in ways which have some seriously socially dysfunctional components. Academic success confers marked benefits on some pupils, but the context in which it is used renders a marked disservice to other individuals and, in some instances, to society.

Other problems have been documented by Schon[5.67] and Nuttgens.[5.68]

As a result of trying—ineffectively—to change the type of education offered to students of management, Schon became acutely aware of some of the barriers to introducing effective (competency-oriented) education. One of these derives from the intrusive, and deeply entrenched, claims of what Schon calls the *technical-rational* model of competence. This he contrasts with a *professional* model of competence. Professional competence, he argues, enables people to cope with unique, complex, uncertain, messy, and changing situations like those which occur in everyday life. It is because educational activities conducted in the tradition of the technical-rational model of competence—ie, that which is most characteristic of modern society—do not foster the competencies that are required to do this that they produce graduates who are incompetent.

What actually happened was that Schon first studied the way in which certain professional groups (architects, town planners, musicians, psychoanalysts) helped their students to develop the competencies they needed to deal with the kinds of problems they typically encounter at work. He and Argyris then tried—for no less than 15 years— to introduce similar activities into management education and other nominally "applied" college programs. Schon attributes their inability to introduce these changes to the claims[5.69] of the dominant technico-rational model of competence. These claims include the belief that competence in modern society is based on a knowledge of content—a belief which contributes to the emphasis which educational institutions place on knowing *that* (things are true) instead of on knowing *how* (to do things). Thus educational institutions place a premium on being articulate and disparage those who are able to do without being able to say why. They emphasize knowledge *of* action rather than (often unverbalized and intuitive) knowledge *in* action. But this is not the only reason why the technical-rational model competence has such a pervasive influence. The model also contributes to, and is reinforced by, the "discipline"-based departmental structure of educational institutions. Whereas (as the arguments about integrated studies show) professional competence is cross-disciplinary, academics gain their significance and are able to advance themselves in their careers almost entirely only by working within "disciplinary" boundaries. They gain the publications on which their careers depend by contributing to the "knowledge"-base of the field rather than by action in the field. They and their students are held accountable for displaying knowledge of content rather than for their ability to tackle any of the problems on which their discipline impinges.

These last observations do not, however, fully explain why the *students* of Schon and Argyris were quite so reluctant to change. Of course, there was a conflict between the competencies they were now being expected to develop and those they had been selected and rewarded for displaying in the past and, indeed, those on which they would probably be graded on at the end of their courses. But it is also entirely possible that their reluctance to engage in these programs is partly explained by their having noted that advancement outside the educational system as much as within it is achieved, not by possessing and displaying any kind of useful competence, but by demonstrating familiarity and facility with fashionable ideas and jargon.

Hogan[5.70] has in fact demonstrated that, while most managers are poised, socially-skilled, extraverted, and intelligent, about a third do actual harm to their organizations as a result of trying to secure their own promotion by doing such things as destroying the developmental potential of their organizations by cutting out the time and the contacts which are required for the network-based activity required to undertake innovative activity, discrediting good people who are potential threats to their own advancement, and failing to tackle organizational problems because doing so would mean that they would have to take unpopular decisions.

Nuttgens[5.71] has developed further the argument that advancement in Western societies (an observation which may, significantly, be less true in Japan) is typically achieved, not by displaying any form of organizational or socially useful competence, but by intoning words and phrases which endear one to one's superiors—and perhaps the public in general. His dominant impression from a lifetime devoted to trying to promote educational change is that the educational system promotes and advances those who are least willing and able to do anything useful and squeezes out those who are willing and able to do so. This comes about because those who are most anxious to be useful are precisely those who can most clearly see that the educational system's claims to convey useful knowledge and foster useful competencies are bogus. (The students squeezed out in this way are not preoccupied with securing prestige and status, so they do not even notice that the system *is* primarily concerned with legitimizing the allocation of these scarce commodities and thus maintaining them in short supply.) The students who remain are those who are least interested in developing, and least able to develop, competencies which are useful for anything other than securing their advancement. He, like Hope,[5.72] notes that they are the ones who are most adept at picking up fashionable words and arranging them up in impressive ways. What he fails to notice is that the main engines of modern economies—their "defence" systems, their "insurance" systems, their "market" systems, and—that largest single industry—their "education and research" systems are equally bogus and depend for their continued operation on being manned by the kinds of people who gain preferment in the "educational" system. The process is, therefore, extremely functional in the short term: our society needs a large number of gullible, double-talking, and/or cynical people who, like priests in the medieval church, mouth high-sounding, but meaningless, phrases either because they naively believe them or because they are cynical enough to secure their own advancement by so doing.

Chomsky[5.73] makes a similar claim. His position is that the educational system promotes intellectuals who perform the function of medieval court jesters. They talk about issues in such a way as to deflect attention from the underlying problems and without challenging the frame in which the problems are set. They use high sounding phrases and give the impression that, because the problem is obviously known to authorities, something will be done about it. In this way they serve to oil the wheels of the system.

Evidence supporting the viewpoint that those who are most willing and able to do useful things drop out of education comes from McClelland's[5.74] much earlier work. This shows that those who are concerned to find new ways of doing things, do or make new things, and make new things happen—ie, those with a high "need" for achievement—ie, those on whom our society is most dependent for innovation—typically leave school early.

Further evidence supporting Chomsky's position comes from Popkewitz[5.75] who suggests that the function of curriculum development activities in education is to entertain the teachers involved and give everyone—public, professionals and pupils alike—the impression that things are getting better when the reality is that things are bad and nearly impossible to change.

The processes which have been described make change in the educational system virtually impossible. The people who remain are least capable of noticing what is going on, least able and willing to do anything about it, and most given to echoing currently fashionable phrases in such a way as to give the impression that those phrases are meaningful and that they are actually going to do something about problems—but often with no understanding of the implications and with little commitment to doing something about them. This makes change increasingly difficult at each successive level in the educational hierarchy...a phenomenon which accords with experience but which is contrary to what the received wisdom about bureaucracy suggests.

In the longer term this system is anything but functional. Not only does the process we have described make change in the educational system itself nearly impossible, it also makes it extremely difficult to initiate the action that is needed to stem the destruction of our planet—the rape of the soils, the seas, the environment, the atmosphere, the poor, and the Third World.

Conclusion

The material summarized in this chapter points to the conclusion that some two thirds of the money spent on secondary education is wasted so far as the development of the talents and competencies of young people is concerned. Schools are, for pupils, the worst working environments in our society. They are also the least developmental. Nevertheless, although highly beneficial to some pupils and to the reproduction of the social order in the short term, the social functions performed by the educational system cannot be other than highly dysfunctional even in the only slightly longer term. They make it almost impossible to initiate rational and innovative action on the basis of good information.

Pupils are **right** to lack enthusiasm for their studies. Schools are not encouraging them to direct their attention to developing important talents. What they are doing confers few developmental benefits on them other than a chance to compete for a privileged position in society. Instead, schools breed a host of dysfunctional beliefs and attitudes. Pupils are right to resist involvement in them. They are right, collectively, to withdraw from competition for norm-referenced grades—because if they all tried harder to reach them, they would all have to run harder to stay in the same place. They would not even get any fitter. They would only become still more exhausted and still more incapable of making their own observations, taking initiative, and inventing better ways of doing things.

CHAPTER 6

HOW DO EFFECTIVE TEACHERS FOSTER HIGH-LEVEL COMPETENCIES?

Over the years we have made a number of studies of the ways in which the development of high-level competencies can be facilitated. Some of these were theoretically-based experiments with managers, employees, teachers and pupils.[6.1] Others involved observations and interviews in homes,[6.2] schools[6.3] and workplaces.[6.4] Our work has been particularly influenced by the research of David McClelland[6.5] and Kohn.[6.6] However, our conclusions are supported by the work of Klemp, Munger and Spencer,[6.7] Huff,[6.8] Gallimore,[6.9] Flanagan,[6.10] Collins,[6.11] Gardner[6.12] and Bachman,[6.13] but most clearly by the work of Jackson[6.14] and Winter, McClelland and Stewart.[6.15]

Before summarizing something of what we observed in schools, it is important to distinguish the activities which will be described from "Progressive Education."

Few advocates for Progressive Education—and particularly the more recent—have been clear about either the distinctive competencies which can be fostered through "progressive education" or the methods to be used to foster them. This is true despite a welter of interesting descriptions of project-based educational activities. Most of these read as if the object of the exercise was to have children discover a mass of low-level everyday **knowledge**[6.16]—when the objective could have been to develop a variety of high-level academic **competencies**—like the ability to make good judgments, make one's own observations, find ways of recording data, or invent ways of communicating feelings or impressions—and unique new knowledge and combinations of specialist knowledge. (Indeed, most of the accounts of the most prestigious work in the area—that occurring at the Lincoln School[6.17]—come across in precisely this way despite the fact that a close reading of the accounts shows that a few of those who organized some of the projects clearly did have other objectives in mind.) This failure to focus on alternative goals has been particularly true of what are perhaps the two largest groups of "Progressive Educators," namely: (1) the "romanticists" who have advocated that form of "child-centered education" in which the child is to be left free to identify and develop his or her own potential (but given little guidance or assistance in doing so), and (2) those who have been so appalled by either or both the personal and social consequences of the competitiveness bred in many schools and the criteria of "academic merit" used to allocate position and status that they have reacted against all explicit objectives and standards. These groups have laid themselves open to the accusation—which Bernstein[6.18] rightly leveled at the "progressive" British Plowden Report—that they were urging teachers to pursue multiple but implicit (or intangible) goals.

What seems to be almost entirely missing is, on the one hand, a theoretically-based account of what we have been calling the motivational dispositions or competencies that are to be fostered through the activities described and, on the other, an account of the *developmental process* itself. For example, it is often emphasized that pupils are to choose the project they will undertake "democratically." However the competencies to be developed in the course of either that "democratic" decision-taking process or in the course of the project itself are rarely spelled out.[6.19]

In the context of what we have so far seen in this book, it is particularly important to note that "Progressive Education" has rarely been portrayed as having distinctive educational *goals*: still less has it been characterized as a highly demanding and structured set of activities which are designed to foster many more important competencies than the low-level-knowledge-oriented activities which dominate traditional classrooms. On the contrary, it has usually been presented as a different *method* of achieving the same goals and, perhaps, equalizing achievement of those goals.[6.20] Furthermore, none of the great men who have written on Progressive Education have followed through into the crucial business of assessment[6.21]—yet no one—teacher or pupil—can pursue multiple, intangible, and unassessable goals very effectively.

I would like American readers to read what follows carefully. Unfortunately, experience shows that the pre-eminence (or hegemony) of the technico-rational formulation of the goals of education leads the majority of American readers to assimilate what is going to be said to the concept of education as "inculcating knowledge" when what I am really saying is something very different. Unless readers understand that I will **not** in this chapter be discussing procedures which are designed to lead to the mastery of **content**, they will not hear what *is* being said. The teachers whose work I will focus on were **not** *primarily* concerned with conveying knowledge of subject matter to their pupils (although they did encourage them to master, and contribute to the development of, high-level specialist knowledge). They were concerned with fostering high-level motivational dispositions or *competencies*.

Just how unusual this approach is may be underlined by noting, first, that there is no reference to such work in the 10-volume *International Encyclopaedia of Education*[6.22] or in the last two editions of the *Handbook of Research on Teaching*.[6.23] Second, by noting that Taylor[6.24] is almost the only American psychologist or educationalist to use the word "learning" to refer to anything other than learning content. Yet there is no reason why it should not be used to refer to learning to do such things as persuade, muster arguments, judge, make good decisions, initiate hunch-based action and use one's feelings to monitor its effects, put others at ease, lead, invent, make one's own observations, develop better ways of thinking about things, or build up one's own understanding of how society works and the willingness and the ability to influence it. Our focus in this chapter is on how children learn to do precisely these things—that is, on how the development of competence to do such things can be fostered.

66

One Teacher's Approach

It is easiest to introduce this work by concentrating for a moment on the work of one teacher who had organized most of her teaching around interdisciplinary, project-based, enquiry-oriented, activity.[6.25] This in itself was extremely unusual: even if project work existed in other classrooms it tended to be viewed as a kind of time-filler or reward, available to those who had "finished their work," at the end of the day.

The project work which this teacher's 8 to 11-year-old pupils undertook within their classroom was an integral part of original enquiries carried out in the environment around the school. These enquiries were organized around a topic, or theme. One such theme covered "The local area and its surroundings." Under this umbrella pupils carried out a number of projects, some individual and some group. One group "project" involved a re-examination of a local archaeological excavation; another, a study of population movements over time, a study of the history of each house and the occupations of its changing occupants, changes in patterns of agriculture, and a study of the current social structure of the area—who was related to whom and what they talked about. All projects involved original research. However, some also involved the initiation of social action—such as getting something done about pollution in the local river. Such a project might be used both as a tool of social research and as a means of promoting the development of the understandings and competencies required to initiate effective social action. Within each project, pupils had personal projects, distinctive areas of specialization, and distinctive roles. Thus one pupil undertook a study of butterflies and their habitats while another studied the history of a hay-rake. The project work which was carried out did not consist—as it so often does—of merely looking material up in reference books—although carrying out an original enquiry or initiating and monitoring some social action might involve tracing and using *specialist* books, research reports, or original accounts of scientific investigations or archaeological excavations. More commonly, if information was wanted, it was obtained by interviewing "ordinary" people or from church records, tombstones, old newspapers, or catalogues unearthed in attics.

But all of this, although extremely unusual, was not what was *most* distinctive about the work of this particular teacher. Most striking were her unusual **concerns**. Like Barnes[6.26] and Curtis,[6.27] she was not preoccupied, as were most teachers, with course work; with covering a syllabus. But neither was she preoccupied with a particular process—such as creating a "democratic" classroom or encouraging an interest in architecture. Instead she focussed *on the high-level* **competencies** which the pupils were to develop **in the course of** *their work.* These competencies included reading, writing, spelling and counting. But they also included communicating, observing, finding the information which was needed to achieve goals (which often had to be collected by observation or by talking to people rather than reading books), inventing, persuading, and leading. In this context even the "3Rs" took on a different complexion. Learning to read, for example, came to include such things as learning to use structure to locate material which might just possibly contain interesting information, learning to use what was read to stimulate lateral thinking, and learning to quickly discard what was not relevant to one's purposes. Writing came to involve such things as the use of allusion and innuendo to influence the reader. Communicating came to include gesture, artwork, diagrams, and body language.

Project work of this kind—though not other kinds of project work—was fairly typical of the relatively small proportion of teachers who successfully nurtured the kinds of competence we have been concerned with in this book. One key feature of the approach was that it enabled them to discover each pupil's distinctive interests and talents. These interests might lie in the types of behavior which made them enthusiastic (such as finding better ways of doing things, getting people to work together, or getting something done about a particular problem [such as pollution]) or they might lie in particular content (such as Celtic civilization or aerodynamics).[6.28] The approach also enabled different pupils to learn to undertake different activities. It confronted the pupils with the fact that there are endless *new* problems out there waiting to be understood and solved: there is no need for them to be put in the position of having to master tired, out-of-date knowledge and the strategies to be used to reproduce solutions to problems which have already been solved. (Incidentally, one great advantage of tackling *new* problems is that the teacher cannot *tell* pupils how to act, but has to show them how to be adventurers, learners, detectives, and discoverers. Another is that unique combinations of up-to-date, high-level, specialist [rather than out-of-date and low-level] knowledge are required if progress is to be made.)

As a result of adopting this approach, it was possible for the teachers to create *developmental environments* in which pupils practiced and developed a selection of high-level competencies (like leadership, initiative, the ability to observe and think, or the ability to understand and influence society) in the course of undertaking activities they cared about.

Since competence involves such things as the willingness to persist for a long period of time in the face of frustration—and often the scorn of others—it was important for the teachers to ensure that the pupils experienced the satisfactions which come from undertaking different sorts of tasks successfully. (Examples include conducting an experiment, putting a group at ease, persuading a local council to change its decisions, or communicating some important ideas to parents.)

In this context the teacher's task was to notice what motivated each pupil, invent an opportunity for the pupil to pursue his or her interests (so that the pupil would, in the process, develop some high-level competencies), monitor the pupil's response to that experience and take corrective action when necessary, and to support the pupils by helping them to tackle problems which would otherwise have discouraged them and led them to give up.

But they did not **only** create opportunities for their pupils to *practice*—and thereby develop—high-level competencies. They also, like good parents and good managers, coached their pupils by creating opportunities for their pupils to see the, normally private, psychological components of competence ... and the consequences. Thus they created opportunities for their pupils to share in their own thinking and prioritizing. They shared their hopes and fears. They talked about their hunches, the auras which excited and beckoned them, the cues which told them when things were going to pay off and when they were going wrong—and thus when corrective action had to be taken. They shared their constant re-formulations of their goals and the problems which needed to be surmounted to reach them—reformulations which occur as a result of (often play-like) rumination and reflection on the effects of hunch-based actions or "experimental interactions with the environment."[6.29] In all these ways they modeled components of competence in such a way that pupils could copy them ... and they let the pupils see that these processes were effective in helping them to reach their goals (and Bandura[6.30] has shown that people are particularly likely to copy effective behaviors).

Some teachers shared their planning and anticipations, their concern with excellence, innovation and efficiency, their disdain for petty regulations, their anticipation of obstacles and their search for ways round them, their concern with aesthetics, and their feeling of being in control of their destinies. They demonstrated how to capitalize upon whatever resources were available—indeed how to select their purposes in the light of the resources that were available and achieve those purposes instead of, as was characteristic of many other teachers, complaining about the lack of resources to do what they wanted to do. In these ways these teachers communicated their values to their pupils and portrayed effective, competent, behavior in such a way that pupils could emulate it. It was not only the overt behavior which was portrayed in this way for the pupils, but the entire pattern of thinking, feeling and striving which normally lies behind it. By deliberately avoiding the role of expert and provider

70

of wisdom—by regularly (and successfully) trying to do things which they themselves did not initially know how to do—they showed their pupils how to be learners and innovators. By demonstrating in their own behavior how thoughts, feelings, and persistence lead to satisfactions that the pupils also wanted, they strengthened the pupils' tendency to engage in the relevant behaviors. They portrayed the strategies of enquiry, anticipation of reactions, and experimentation which are required to build up an understanding of a complex biophysical or social process, the strategies required to intervene in it, anticipate the way aspects of the system would react, and take corrective action when necessary. By accepting pupils' suggestions, they showed them that authorities and leaders are not best regarded as sources of information and organization, but as people who, at best, help other people to articulate and share what they know, acknowledge what others have contributed, and lead others to feel capable of achieving, and to be motivated to achieve their own goals.

Some of these teachers, like some parents, realized that, if pupils are to learn from mentors who portray the cognitive, affective, and conative components of high-level competence, mentor and disciple must share at least some of their enthusiasms, talents and concerns.[6.31] Since there is no possibility that a single teacher's values could mesh with those of all his or her pupils, they realized that it was essential to place children with other adults outside the school who shared their values and to engage a range of other adults with them in the class's activities so that pupils could see people successfully exercising important components of competence while undertaking activities which they (the pupils) cared about. They also used stories, literature, and historical material to illuminate the intra-psychic, cognitive, affective, and conative components of competence, and illustrate the personal and social consequences of pursuing different kinds of valued activity, and deploying different patterns of competence, in different types of society having different institutional arrangements and dominant cultural concerns. (One might add that they could, with advantage, also have prepared case history materials and materials derived from psychological research for this purpose).

In a similar way their pupils learned a great deal from, and came to rely more extensively on, their fellow pupils. They developed a partnership in learning. Aided by a vocabulary supplied by their teachers, they became able to think about, and value, the contributions of others. The teachers would encourage them to identify the particular talents and contributions of their fellows and enlist their help in trying to find ways of tapping the energies of other—perhaps in some ways disruptive—pupils. In this way the teachers helped their pupils to develop and use multiple-talent concepts of competence and ability instead of classifying their fellows only as "smart" or "dumb." They made explicit both the fact that not everyone contributes in the same way to a group process, and also to the thought processes which contribute to effective leadership and management; ie, to the processes which are involved in identifying, developing, and using the talents of each member of the work group. By engaging their pupils in this process the teachers therefore helped them to develop the competencies required for effective leadership and management.

Many of these observations have been confirmed by Jackson.[6.32] But he also noticed something which, in retrospect, was also true of the effective teachers we studied but which we failed to comment upon. This was that teachers who had the effect of transforming pupils by releasing new competencies were unusually likely to read parable-like stories to their pupils.

High Schools and Higher Education

While these examples come from elementary schools, we have observed the same things in high schools,[6.33] and Winter, McClelland and Stewart,[6.34] in an outstanding study of Ivy League and other colleges in the United States, have described the same processes at this level and documented their consequences for the future lives of those concerned and the communities in which they lived. The course content is not important. Neither is residential experience. What is important is participating in challenging activities which demand high-levels of initiative, self-reliance, leadership, and specialist knowledge and exposure to mentors who portray the thoughts, feelings, and behaviors which are characteristic of competent people. So is experience of the satisfactions which come from having undertaken a difficult and demanding activity. However, just as only a few elementary or high schools provide the kind of experiences we have described, so Winter *et al* demonstrated that few universities do so either.[6.35]

Toward an Understanding of Some of the Barriers

We will now go over some of the same ground again, but this time in a way which will help us to identify some of the barriers to the dissemination of such work.

As has been mentioned, one of the pupils in one of the schools we visited had become an expert on the distribution of different species of butterfly in the locality and their dependence at various stages in their life cycles on features of local habitats. Another had become an expert on the history of a hay-rake: how it had changed over time and how those changes were related to developments in steel making on the one hand and patterns of land use on the other. A third had become an expert on the social structure of the area around the school: who knew whom, and what they talked about.

It would be hard to give students credit for such unique specialist knowledge using traditional tests; separate tests would be required to identify each child's knowledge.

But this is the least of the problems which this work poses for assessment. More important than the unique store of specialist knowledge built up by the first pupil mentioned above was the fact that he had developed a selection of the *competencies* which are required to be a scientist. Among other things, he had learned to be sensitive to the cues which told him that he had an unresolved problem. He had developed the tendency to try to make glimmers of insight on the fringe of consciousness explicit. He would wake up at night in an effort to do so. He had strengthened his tendency to do these things—and his confidence that he could do them—as a result of experiencing the satisfactions which come from noticing, and beginning to understand, things which no one had noticed or understood before. He had contacted university lecturers who were interested in the same problem and spoken to them as equals. He had sharpened up his ideas by sparring with them. He had learned not only that he had a right to ask questions and that his questions were as good as those posed by others, but also that he had a right to expect others to help him answer them. He had learned to tolerate the frustrations which are involved in trying to find better ways of thinking about things. He had learned to find ways of summarizing his insights—not only in words, but also in diagrams and mathematical formulae.[6.36]

The second pupil had developed the self-motivated competencies, preoccupations, sensitivities, thoughtways, and perceptions required to be a historian. And the third had developed the competencies required to be a sociologist. And so on for the other pupils. Each had developed some of the competencies required to perform effectively in one or another of the wide range of jobs and roles (including wife, husband, mother, or cook) required in modern society.

Existing assessment procedures are even less able to document the growth of the subtle skills, motivated habits, thoughtways and preoccupations which contribute to this repertoire of competencies required by the scientist, historian, sociologist, photographer, cook, or mother than they are to cope with the problem of idiosyncratic knowledge.

Even this does not exhaust the problems which the educational process we have described pose for evaluation and certification. Because the pupils had worked as a group, one pupil had become good at coordinating the activities of others, another at putting others at ease and smoothing over difficulties, another at presenting the results of other people's work to external visitors—a communicator rather than a scientist. In the course of doing these things all pupils learned to communicate, to invent, to make their own observations, to work with others, and to lead and to follow. These competencies defy conventional measurement.

As we shall see in the next chapter, this measurement problem is of particular importance partly because teachers teach and pupils work toward the goals that are *assessed*, partly because, in order to improve their performance, teachers and pupils need means of monitoring progress toward these goals, and partly because teachers need some tools to help them to administer multiple, individualized, competency-oriented, educational programs. Yet assessing these qualities poses a host of dilemmas.

Concluding Comment

It is important to conclude this chapter by first reemphasizing that the competency-oriented educational process which has been briefly described is quite different both from the content-oriented educational programs which dominate American, English, and Scottish schools and from the activities which have been pursued under the rubric of "Progressive Education" in America.[6.37] *The objective of the teachers whose work has been summarized was to nurture high-level competencies like the ability to lead, invent, make one's own observations, and find ways of summarizing them.* In contrast to this, most "Progressive Education" has remained heavily *content*-oriented. Indeed, the hegemony of the notion that education is *the same thing as* acquisition of knowledge of content prevents many readers even hearing what has been said in this chapter. What is involved can best be highlighted by saying that the change in orientation that is needed involves a shift from teaching as telling to teaching as facilitating growth and a shift from content-oriented to competency-oriented education. If we are to promote movement in these directions it will be necessary to place much more emphasis on differentiation and variety in the educational system, but doing so creates problems to which we will turn in the next chapter.

CHAPTER 7

WHY DO SCHOOLS NEGLECT THEIR MAIN GOALS?

It may be thought that schools' lack of attention to the wider goals of education is adequately explained by the lack of clarity about the goals that are to be achieved and how they are to be achieved, the difficulties involved in nurturing the desired qualities, the dearth of ways of monitoring their development, and the absence of means of recording the outcomes in ways that are acceptable in the certification and placement process.[7.1] In fact, further serious problems arise from the value-based nature of competence and the social functions which the educational system performs for society. These will be reviewed in this chapter.

The Problem is not a Lack of Time, Money, Resources or Teacher Training

Before moving on it is important to note that the significant barriers to educational reform do not include a lack of time, money, resources, traditional support staff, conventional forms of teacher training, or accepted forms of staff development.

Progressive Education in America has a long history of well-funded and well-resourced attempts to tackle the problems which confront the educational system. These include those of Dewey,[7.2] Aikin,[7.3] Caswell,[7.4] and the Newton School System.[7.5] Fraley[7.6] has shown that billions of dollars, and endless teacher and support time, together with ample professional assistance from university staff, were poured into seven US school systems. Despite this, at least once the external support and limelight was withdrawn, only about 5% of teachers did what it was hoped they would do.

In Britain, numerous attempts, each costing millions of dollars, have been made to reform the educational system in ways which would lead it to focus on the goals we have been concerned with in this book. These have included the introduction of mixed ability teaching (which was, in part, designed to stimulate the invention of ways of identifying and fostering more of the talents of more of the pupils and to focus attention on ways of fostering talents which are more important than those designated as "academic" in most schools), some of the curriculum development projects of the sixties and seventies,[7.7] and the introduction of profiles and records of achievement (which were intended to enable pupils to get recognition for a wider range of talents and thus legitimize more broadly based programs of education).[7.8] None of these "initiatives" met with notable success ... yet they are now being joined by a number of other well funded "developments." One is the Technical and Vocational Education Initiative. This is explicitly intended to foster qualities like initiative, the ability to communicate, the ability to work with others, problem solving ability, and the ability to understand society.[7.9] Despite its goals, however, the programs rarely include the kinds of activity that would be needed to nurture such competencies. Another is the attempt, embedded in the Education Reform Bill,[7.10] to improve education by specifying curriculum content, introducing regular testing of pupils and teachers, devolving some powers to school boards, and offering parents a choice of school in the context of published performance data.[7.11] Both programs have been accompanied by huge development exercises based on the assumption that the problem and the solution were correctly diagnosed and understood—but by virtually no fundamental research of the kind we have been concerned with in this book.

Class size is often blamed for some of the problems. Yet the IEA data[7.12] show that teachers with small classes generally pursue the same goals, and teach in the same way, as those with larger classes. Dewey had one adult to every four pupils in his experimental school—but still only about 5% of the teachers did what he enjoined them to do. In a pre-school Home Visiting project which we evaluated, teachers (who were also mothers) worked with *individual* children for an hour a week over about 9 months. Few of them facilitated the development of high-level competencies in these children in the way in which they themselves—in their role as mothers—facilitated their development in their own children.

Lack of resources, large classes, and time for conventional development work are, therefore, not the main barriers to the dissemination of the kind of work undertaken by the outstanding teachers whose work was summarized in Chapter 6. Several unsuspected, and much more serious, barriers have, however, come to light in the course of our work. These will be discussed in this chapter under nine headings.

(1) The absence of tools to help teachers to manage multiple, individualized, competency-oriented programs of education

Running competency-oriented educational programs is a difficult, creative, inventive, and frustrating job: As indicated earlier, teachers have to find out what each pupil cares about and is good at, invent a range of personalized developmental programs which enable pupils to practice (and thereby develop) some of the wide range of competencies which might be developed and which are needed in society, monitor pupils' reactions to those experiences, and take corrective action when necessary. When there are 30 or more students in a class, this is an almost superhuman task. We have found that those teachers who do manage it have painstakingly—and often at considerable personal cost—developed the necessary sensitivities, monitoring strategies, and competencies over many—perhaps 20—years.[7.13] If more teachers are to do what these outstanding teachers appear to do "instinctively," it will be necessary for them to have some tools which will help them to undertake the activities mentioned above explicitly. Those tools will have to enable them to identify each pupil's motives or values, indicate personalized developmental programs for each pupil, and familiarize them (the teachers) with the concepts they need to think about multiple talents and their development.[7.14]

(2) The absence of means of giving pupils or teachers credit, in the certification and placement process, for having developed high-level competencies

The next problem is the absence of appropriate summative assessment procedures. To understand the importance of this, we must first recall that we have already seen that most pupils and parents know that the main benefit offered by the "educational" system is not education at all. It is grade-bearing credentials or certificates which will buy entry to courses of further and higher education and thereafter entry to protected occupations.[7.15] They are therefore faced with a dilemma if they are offered programs which are genuinely developmental but which do not lead to tradable certificates.[7.16] Teachers have a similar dilemma. They would be jeopardizing their pupils' life-chances if they offered them programs which nurtured important high-level competencies but which, by taking time away from the syllabi on which they will be tested, reduced their chances of obtaining high grades. Perhaps just as importantly, since teachers' reputations are based on their ability to ensure that their students get high grades, they would be jeopardizing their own prospects as well.

It is for these reasons that it is what is assessed in the certification and placement process—and not the educational aspirations of parents, pupils, teachers, curriculum councils, secretaries of education or anyone else—which primarily determines what happens in schools.[7.17] Teachers would generally prefer not to recognize this sociological reality or address the dilemmas it poses.[7.18] Many of them come into teaching because they want to help people and do a worthwhile job in the community.[7.19] They resent—and are demeaned by— the child-minding and social-allocative roles which society thrusts upon them. Rather than think about how the sociological imperative that schools allocate position and status might be grasped and satisfied, they want someone else (such as employers or the universities) to perform these tasks and leave them free to get on with education. Unfortunately, Dore's[7.20] data shows that this is sociologically naive: Teachers' behavior continues to be determined by what is assessed in the certification and placement process—regardless of how widely its irrelevance is acknowledged and regardless of who does the assessing.

Actually, ways of assessing these qualities are not only needed for certification purposes. They are also needed if teachers and pupils are to be able to monitor progress toward important goals and obtain the feedback needed to improve their performance—and, indeed, if they are to know that they have accomplished anything worthwhile in the time they have devoted to the necessary activities. Means of assessing such qualities are equally badly needed for use in evaluation studies and accountability exercises. If no such measures are available, the educational system's failure to achieve its main goals will continue to be unknown on the "factual" register which largely determines the educational policy-making agenda. So long as this is known only "intuitively"—in the way it is currently known to parents, teachers, pupils and employers—it does not figure in the discussions which determine educational policy. Proposals to improve education will continue to focus on the easily measurable, but relatively trivial, and miss the important (witness the way in which the educational-improvement-through-testing philosophy has swept the world).

(3) The conflict between the procedures which are required to foster high-level competencies and the widely held view that "teaching" *means* "telling"

The activities which are required to nurture the development of high-level competencies are best captured by the term "facilitating growth."[7.21] Yet, overlooking the fact that fostering the abilities required to read, write and count involves advancing skills or competencies, most people believe that teaching is about "telling"—transmitting *information* from teachers to pupils.

81

This identity between education and "telling" on the one hand, and knowing the "right" things to say on the other, has resulted in a vicious circle: Teaching as a profession recruits a disproportionate number of people who want to be the center of attention and the source of wisdom[7.22] ... and these are exactly the sort of teachers that many pupils and students think they want. Those who have the skills and sensitivities which are required to facilitate growth tend not to become teachers in the first place, and they are often rejected by their students if they do find their way into teaching. The conflict between the satisfactions which most teachers want from teaching and the satisfactions available to those who facilitate development— even in language laboratories—results in many teachers finding such activities so distressing that they corrupt them back into "telling."

What these observations show is that there is a serious conflict between the role required of teachers if they are to facilitate the development of competence and:

(i) parents', pupils', and students' accurate observation that the "educational" system is not mainly about developing competence but about legitimizing the rationing of privilege and teaching people how to buy personal advancement by ingratiating themselves with their superiors, and

(ii) the satisfactions which teachers want from their jobs.

If progress is to occur, it will be necessary to get this conflict out into the open and ensure that it is carefully addressed.

If more emphasis is to be placed on facilitating the growth of competence, it will also be necessary to challenge another widely held belief which derives from the technical-rational model of competence. This is that "learning" can be chopped up into 40-minute "periods" or 40-hour "modules." The work we have reviewed shows that high-level competencies are usually developed while people are involved in difficult and demanding activities that they care about, which continue over an extended period of time, and which lead, in the end, to something worthwhile (thus enabling those concerned to experience the benefits and satisfactions which come from having engaged in such difficult and demanding activities).[7.23]

(4) The problems which stem from the *transformational* nature of the educational activities which are required to foster high-level competencies

To promote the development of high-level competencies, one starts by studying pupils' motives and incipient talents. One then tries to invent individualized developmental experiences which will test one's initial hypotheses about incipient interests and talents and the processes which will lead them to flower.[7.24] One cannot know the outcome of this process in advance. One may end up doing things which are quite different to those one initially envisaged. Unexpected talents surface and develop. In this way pupils are *transformed*.[7.25] All of this is fine from an educational point of view. But it is in sharp conflict with widely held beliefs about the ways in which it is appropriate to spend public money. It is generally believed that one should not take risks with such money and that contractors (teachers or researchers) should be able to specify in advance what the results of the expenditure will be. Funding an *adventure* which may (or may not) transform people or existing understandings is viewed as not merely risky; it is illegitimate. The solution to this problem has not only to do with legitimizing venturesome activity in the public sector. It also involves finding ways of identifying the sorts of teachers who are able to capitalize on what they stumble across in the course of an adventure—ie, teachers who are able to recognize the value of something they have come upon "by chance" and turn it to advantage. To do this it will be necessary to develop staff appraisal tools which will make it possible to identify, recognize, reward, and encourage among teachers the very competencies that we have been concerned with in this book.

(5) The dilemmas associated with catering for diversity

We have seen that high-level competencies can only be nurtured when people are doing things they care about, and that this means tailoring developmental tasks to pupils' personal values, priorities, and motives. It is sometimes impossible for pupils to pursue goals which they care about in the same room as other pupils undertake tasks which *they* care about. For example, one cannot, in the same classroom, meet the needs of those pupils who want to develop toughness and strength and those who wish to develop the sensitivities required to learn how to set their minds to the "dreamy" state required to notice the fleeting feelings on the fringe of consciousness which form the germ of nearly all creative insights and slowly bring them to the center of attention so that they become articulate and communicable.

This need for variety and choice conflicts with the widely accepted emphasis on equality and uniformity in public provision—uniformity which is stressed in such developments as the English National Curriculum. It is therefore essential to make explicit, and possibly challenge, the reasons for this distaste for variety in the public domain. One of its causes is the experience-based belief that such variety leads to a *hierarchy* of options—running from those which are of high quality to those which are poor—rather than to alternatives which are very different from each other, but all of which are of high quality. When the quality of provision varies only from good to bad, the more informed, articulate, and powerful tend to get the best deal. It was, indeed, to counteract just this tendency that education was brought into the public domain in the first place. If the stultifying effects of the emphasis on equality in public provision are to be reduced, it will therefore be necessary to introduce much more effective quality control mechanisms to both (*i*) document the personal and social consequences of each of a number of demonstrably different options, and (*ii*) assure the public that each option is of high quality.

Another objection to providing variety and choice in public education is the fear that it will lead to the ossification, even exacerbation, of class differences in the social structure. Fortunately, the evidence already summarized in this book does not support these fears: In the first place, a wide variety of different patterns of competence is required in modern society. Even a single occupational group requires people who want do very different things and who possess different patterns of competence. Secondly, no one person could possibly develop all the concerns and patterns of competence we have identified in the course of our work.[7.26] Thirdly, pupils have very different preoccupations, concerns, and talents: they want very different things from their education and very different satisfactions from their work.[7.27] Fourthly, this variation is more closely related to the occupational destinations pupils are bound for than to their social origins.[7.28] Fifthly, there is, in our society, a great deal more intergenerational social mobility—both upward and downward—than people believe.[7.29] The picture is therefore much more complex than has often been suggested, and it points very strongly toward the need to respect, and build on, the variance in pupils' values, priorities, and patterns of competence instead of "inculcating middle-class values into working-class children." The specter of teachers perpetuating socio-economic divisions and creating a caste society if they treat different children in different ways does not seem to be well founded.

(6) Value conflicts

A host of serious problems flow from the fact that high-level competencies are heavily value-laden and involve social and political beliefs.[7.30]

The first is that any teacher who attempts to foster them is invariably confronted by parents and pupils who either do not value (*i*) the competencies (such as the tendency to ask questions or the ability to find information for oneself) which it is hoped to foster or (*ii*) the activities the teacher hopes to initiate to allow his or her pupils to practice, and thereby develop, such competencies. (For example, a teacher might plan to nurture a range of high-level competencies by encouraging his or her class to try to stop a factory polluting a local river—an activity which would almost certainly lead to objections from some parents.[7.31])

There are several reasons why this problem cannot be simply resolved by offering the public a variety of programs which are tailored to different values and which aim to foster alternative talents. Among them are:

(i) As we have noted, the idea that teachers should treat different children in different ways conflicts with the current emphasis on equality in public provision.

(ii) Even parents who are basically in favor of schools fostering high-level competencies are faced by the dilemma that working at such activities will take time away from subject-and-grade-oriented activity and is thus likely to jeopardize their life chances. However, a related problem is that many parents who do want their children to enjoy the economic and social benefits which are associated with high status managerial jobs do not want their children to do some things that it is necessary for them to do to develop the competencies which are required to perform those jobs effectively. For example, managerial ability involves the ability to ask pertinent questions: Yet many parents do not want their children to ask questions—particularly if it would mean that they themselves would have to justify their commands. Another important competence is the ability to venture into the unknown—yet many parents cannot tolerate the anxieties which arise when children undertake tasks which are on the verge of their capabilities.[7.32] A still more fundamental problem is that many parents (and teachers) know that they themselves lack the competencies which are required to manage independent, adventurous, children who take initiative, think for themselves, and guide their behavior by reference to personalized, reason-based, moral codes.

(*iii*) Many parents not only do not, on balance, want schools to foster high-level competencies in their own children, they do not want them to nurture them in other people's children either: If they did, those other children would do better in life than their own. This is why so many people oppose private schools even when they would not send their own children to them even if they could. Private schools can, and often do, inculcate important values and political beliefs—and foster important value-based competencies. But any public school which attempted to do the same would be engulfed in a political furor.

The net effects of the processes just described are, firstly, that the ethos of public schools is more correctly described as *working-class* than "middle-class," and, secondly that, cumulatively, they make change extraordinarily difficult. Thus while, in the end, the solution to the problems posed by the value-laden nature of high-level competencies will have to come through offering pupils and parents a variety of demonstrably different educational programs, the provision of variety is not sufficient in itself. It will also be necessary to surface and challenge many social and civic beliefs and resolve some of the dilemmas identified above.

To resolve those dilemmas it will be necessary to:

(*i*) Systematically generate a range of educational programs which will appeal to people with very different concerns and incipient talents and which will lead them to develop very different concerns and patterns of competence.

(*ii*) Accumulate much better research data on the differential consequences of each of the alternatives for the pupils concerned and for the societies in which they live. (Such data should include information on the consequences of each option be for: (a) the patterns of life-satisfaction and competence the pupils develop at the

87

time, (b) the career options open to the pupils in the future, (c) the patterns of life satisfaction and frustration that those concerned are likely to experience in the future [in the context of alternative changes in society], and (d) societal change itself.)

(*iii*) Develop the tools and structures which are needed to (a) assure the public that the options, although distinctly different, are all of high quality, and (b) administer that variety equitably.

It follows from these observations that, if the public is to be offered a variety of options which have very different consequences and be invited to choose between them, we will need to run our society very differently. Among other things, the public service will have to: (*i*) invent, and provide in each community, a variety of options, and (*ii*) collect, and provide people with, the information they need to choose between those options.

What this means is that the public service will need to feed information *outwards* to the public, rather than upwards through bureaucratic hierarchy to elected representatives who take decisions *for* the public. This will in effect mean that the main decision makers will be the public, not elected representatives.

The task of supervising the information collected and disseminated at each level will require much greater public and media involvement. If this is to happen we will need a much more transparent public bureaucracy, changed roles for elected representatives, and changed citizenship activities. Put another way, we will need to develop new, network-based, participative (rather than representative) forms of democracy to monitor and influence the public service.

It appears, therefore, that (*i*) fundamental research directed toward the solution of these practical problems, (*ii*) a wide range of development activities, and (*iii*) programs of adult civic education to promote the evolution of new means of managing society are unexpected prerequisites to effective schooling. It follows that one of the first steps to be undertaken by schools is, somewhat surprisingly, to change the beliefs they lead their pupils to adopt about the procedures which are required to promote social development.

A second problem posed by the value-laden nature of competence is that fostering important competencies means influencing pupils' values and political, economic, and civic beliefs. This raises the specter of brainwashing. Once again, the dilemmas which this poses are most likely to be resolved by finding ways of making what is going on more visible, by providing more markedly different options, and by providing better information on the long term personal and social consequences of each of the alternatives.

But there is a still more thorny issue to be addressed. We have not only argued that all important competencies are value-based but also that the effective operation of both our educational system and our staff guidance, placement, and development systems is dependent on the *assessment* of these value-laden qualities. The specter of explicitly assessing value-based motivational dispositions for these purposes throws the moral questions associated with educators working in this area into sharp relief. One can only respond that it would be better to do it openly than do it clandestinely.

(7) The barriers posed by the latent functions of the educational system

In Chapter 5 we saw that the educational system: (*i*) nurtures the tendency to work out which behavior one's superiors will favor and do whatever is necessary to secure one's preferment regardless of the consequences for one's organization or society,[7.33] (*ii*) breeds that kind of facility with words that enables people to create a good impression by using fashionable phrases, (*iii*) advances those who are best able to do these things, (*iv*) squeezes out those who are most anxious to act in the long term interests of society and those who are best able to invent new ways of thinking about and doing things, (*v*) selects those who are, because of personal ambition or naivety, most willing and

able to undertake the fraudulent "work" of modern society, and
(*vi*) operates to perpetuate an inequitable society by legitimizing
the way in which privilege is rationed instead of fostering and
promoting those best able to identify and introduce changes in the
way society is organized. We concluded that these processes
make it very difficult to change what happens in schools.

We may now introduce yet another observation about the
functioning of the educational system. This is that the way in
which it works reflects the way modern societies work. To substantiate this claim we must first examine some features of the
way contemporary society works. Despite its rhetoric, the main
things manufactured by the marketplace are: (*i*) useless jobs, and
(*ii*) discriminations which compel participation in the make-work
activities of which modern society is largely composed. It is
easiest to see this by considering the insurance industry. Insurance should be a simple matter of transferring resources from
those who have them to those who do not. In fact, the insurance
industry manufactures endless jobs and magnifies differences between the rich and the moderately rich in such a way as to compel participation in the system. Thus the industry creates jobs for
endless people generating insurance packages, selling those packages, collecting and keeping account of small sums of money,
assessing entitlement, pursuing legal wrangles, assessing the
profitability of companies in which it might be suitable for the
insurance company to invest, investing in those companies,
monitoring those investments, and intervening in the companies
concerned. It also generates crass differences between the
benefits available to those who can pay and those who are sub-
jected to degrading and dehumanizing treatment because, although they have the greatest need, are unable to pay. The
educational system works in much the same way: It offers activities which occupy a lot of time of a lot of people; it creates
jobs for teachers, administrators, researchers, publishers,
librarians, editors and test agencies; it manufactures discriminations between individuals whose competence differs only slightly; it makes use of norm-referenced assessments which require
more people to spend more time in the system to attain the same

occupational position; and it promotes and advances those who are most concerned with their personal advancement and least concerned with, able to analyze, and anxious to do something about, wider social problems. This parallel between the educational system and society was not discussed in Chapter 5 because we were there concerned with the educational and human resource components of the educational system. The processes we are describing here are purely sociological...but they clearly contribute to the difficulties involved in introducing change.

This is not, however, the only way in which the educational system seems socially functional in the short term but dysfunctional in the longer term: The system also operates as if it were designed to lay the blame for the ills of society at the door of the uneducated and those who are least able to do anything about those social problems instead of at the door of the leaders and managers of society. In the same way, the "devolution of management and control" procedures currently being widely advocated for the educational system throughout the world seem designed to lay the blame for the ills of the educational system on teachers and parents rather than on the administrators and politicians who could do something about them: teachers and parents are in no position to do anything about the social constraints on what schools and teachers can do, to alter the tests which are inflicted on schools in any fundamental way, to influence the text books that get written, or to generate the understandings and tools which are required to run alternative educational programs.

The parallel between what the educational system does in this respect and what the IMF does on a grander scale should not be overlooked: just as current social and educational policies tend to legitimize blaming the poor for their poverty, so the IMF blames poor people in poor countries for their poverty instead of the leaders of those countries and those who are responsible for managing the international financial system—namely bankers, international public servants, politicians, and the managers of trans-national corporations.

91

Perhaps the most insidious aspect of the educational system is that it nurtures the tendency to go along with things that are not what they seem to be and promotes those who are most willing to quote the conventional wisdom despite its lack of reference to reality. Thus the educational system advances those who are least willing to notice that the educational system is not what it seems or claims to be. Such people are, in the short term, ideally suited to jobs in insurance, the World Bank, "aid" agencies, welfare agencies, the public service, the food industry, and politics and government. The most pervasive, but least remarked, feature of modern society is that **nothing** is what it seems to be—and is, in fact, usually its opposite.[7.34] The tendency of the educational system to disseminate false consciousness and promote those most inclined to engage in "double talk" makes it extremely difficult to conduct any rational discussion of wider social processes.

Although it is tempting to see some kind of conspiracy in the parallelism between what happens in the educational system and the wider society and in the educational system's tendency to introduce false consciousness into discussions of social processes when these threaten the short term interests of those with more power in society, it is not necessary to make that assumption. The educational system has grown on the basis of myths. These include: "If we all get more education we'll all get good jobs" and "More education will make for economic and social development."[7.35] It has also grown as a result of the less mythical fact that, whatever doubts there may be about the educational benefits of the system, staying on at school confers a greater likelihood of obtaining a good job. Despite these observations, Robinson's[7.36] discovery that there *was* a very effective conspiracy to discredit the work of Harold Rugg is disconcerting. Because Rugg's books were *effective* in fostering in pupils the tendency and ability to think critically about the workings of society, the National Association of Manufacturers mounted a deliberate campaign to discredit both Rugg and his books—a campaign from which he never recovered. The documents which Robinson has reviewed show beyond reasonable doubt that this involved numerous accusations which were known to be false and deliberate lying to congressional committees of enquiry. It is hard to believe that work as innocuous as Rugg's—directed toward what is widely agreed to be one of the main goals of education—could have produced such concerted, sustained, dirty tricks. Robinson's (and Bellini's[7.37])work therefore leads one to take more seriously the claims of those, like Chomsky,[7.38] who are inclined toward the conspiracy theory.

If these observations are correct, it is obvious that it would be extremely difficult to do such things as introduce any form of multiple talent education designed to develop and credential at least some of the talents of all of our children—because this would undermine the educational system's role in manufacturing and legitimizing discriminations of a kind which would compel participation in institutional arrangements which give meaning to life in modern society.

That this hypothesis is not so far-fetched as it may at first sight appear to be can be seen by reflecting on what happened to attempts to reform examinations in England and Wales. For 20 years, committees of the (national) Schools Council for Curriculum and Examinations debated the desirability of establishing a common system of examinations without coming to a conclusion. Then the Minister for Education established a new committee with a specific remit to come to a conclusion. The committee observed that pupils had a wide variety of talents which could only be fostered through very different types of educational programs. It noted that workplaces and society required a wide variety of people who possessed very different talents. It therefore concluded that there was a need for a wide variety of educational programs which would foster very different competencies and in the course of which pupils would cover very different syllabi. This led it to the conclusion that it would be necessary to retain a wide variety of examining boards (the equivalent of ETS and ACTS) which would each promote a wide variety of courses covering different content, aim at different goals, and be assessed using different forms, or "modes," of assessment. Then it did something which was, at first sight, inexplicable. In one sentence, embedded in a long paragraph, it said, "the results will be expressed on a single scale of seven points in the subject area." This, of course, negated all the steps—based on all the educational and occupational observations it had made—that it planned to make to promote and cater for diversity. If one asks oneself what could have caused such an action, one can only conclude that the sociological need for a single and unarguable criterion to legitimize the allocation of position and status—and with it a whole social system for rationing privilege—had over-ridden all human, educational, and occupational considerations.

What all this means is that, if education is to be brought back into schools, those concerned (including teachers), will *as part of their professional duties deriving from their remit to achieve educational goals,* have to take active steps to influence the way society is organized.

(8) Dysfunctional beliefs about the role of the public servant.

We have seen that competency-oriented education requires teachers to pay attention to the needs of individual pupils and to invent individualized developmental programs which will lead them to blossom. It also requires them to get together with other teachers to invent better ways of meeting pupils' needs, to find ways of influencing the tests which are available from test publishers (so that these cease to direct attention toward low-level goals and away from high-level goals), and to influence the beliefs which parents and others hold about education itself and the way the public service in general should operate. Unfortunately, teachers, like other public servants, are not generally expected to be inventors and activists of this sort. They are viewed as functionaries who should do the bidding of elected representatives. To solve this problem we not only need to re-think our beliefs about how the public service should operate and to create structures (*a la* Kanter[7.39]) which promote innovation, we also need to apply new criteria to judge the effectiveness of public servants and to develop new tools for use in staff appraisal—so that teachers can get credit for engaging in the difficult, demanding, frustrating, and time-consuming activities which are required if they are to do their jobs effectively. The way in which this is to be done will be discussed in the next chapter.

(9) The absence of an innovative educational system

In the course of this book, we have seen that the attempt to deal with the conspicuous problems of the educational system by trying to prescribe what children will learn and then find out whether they have learned it using centrally prescribed tests of the traditional type is misguided. We have seen that the barriers to effective education are deep-seated and non-obvious, that what children need to learn to do varies markedly from pupil to pupil, that the available tests are unable to reflect the high-level competencies which students need to develop, and that our hierarchical management system has been unable even to eliminate grossly incompetent teachers, never mind to create a ferment of innovation. Pervasive innovation in every nook and cranny of the educational system is required. There is no way in which any central authority can lay down what teachers will do, never mind prescribe what individual children should learn. Instead, the task of a central authority is to create a structure and set of expectations which will: (*i*) lead to increasing clarity about the goals which are to be achieved and the procedures which are to be used to reach them; (*ii*) encourage all concerned to assess whether they are achieving their goals effectively; (*iii*) encourage them to identify the barriers to success; and (*iv*) lead them to vigorously set about trying to do something about those barriers.

It is clear from these observations that one of the barriers to the evolution and diffusion of educational innovations has to do with the fact that the educational system operates in the context of a set of beliefs to the effect that it is the job of publicly elected representatives and senior management both to establish the goals of the educational system and the procedures to be used to reach them—with its corollary that the teacher's job is to carry out the

95

activities prescribed by such authorities. These beliefs and expectations discourage teachers from studying the needs of their pupils and trying to invent better ways of meeting them. Unfortunately, these beliefs are only part of a much wider problem: In Britain and the United States, since innovation is thought to be the prerogative of management, the educational system does not have a management structure which stimulates and facilitates innovation. We have already seen that the stimulation of innovation involves creating within the educational system what Kanter has called "parallel organization" activity which would focus on innovation. What we are now saying is that we also need to replace our hierarchical management structures—our structures of bureaucracy and democracy—by network based management structures of the kind advocated by Toffler,[7.40] Schon[7.41] and Ferguson.[7.42] These will be discussed more fully in Chapter 9. Here it is sufficient to note that the failure to create an innovative educational system is not only dysfunctional in itself—it also has the gravest knock-on effect on society as a whole because teachers powerfully communicate to their pupils their own beliefs about what it is important to attend to and how things should be done.[7.43]

We may conclude by noting that what has been said implies that the areas in which research and innovation are *most* badly needed in our society do *not* have to do with finding better ways of producing goods of one kind or another but with finding better ways of running society itself. The way in which such research is to be organized will be discussed in Chapter 10.

Summary

Following Morgan,[7.44] Diagram 1 has been prepared to summarize what we have now learned about the feedback loops which result in, and reinforce, narrow educational activity. It shows how the narrow nature of educational provisions is heavily over-determined and demonstrates why it has been so difficult to introduce change in education. The effects of any single change

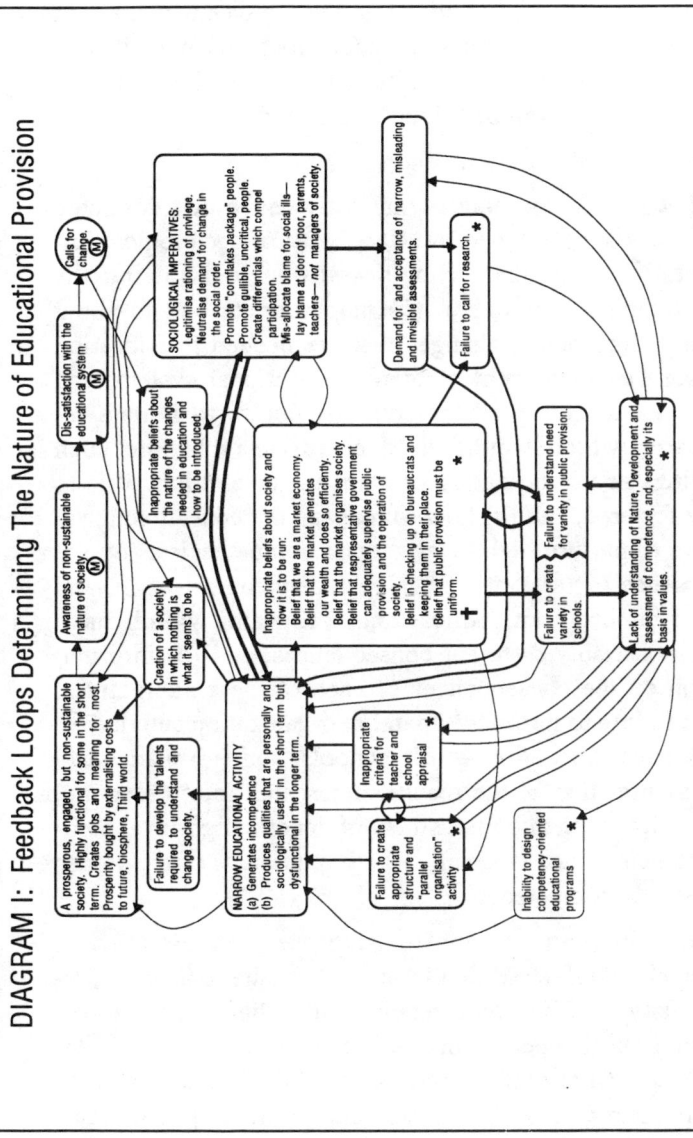

DIAGRAM I: Feedback Loops Determining The Nature of Educational Provision

* Intervention in these cells would help change the nature of the qualities nurtured and rewarded in the system. Motives which should be harnessed to do this are marked Ⓜ.

†These need to be replaced by acceptance of the need to make managed economies work—to find ways of giving effect to information concerning the public long term interest, the need to explicitly create variety and information on the personal and social consequences of the options, and to find ways of holding public servants accountable for, and getting them to act in, the long term public interest. This means systematic, broadly-based, evaluation and participative democracy.

6 Jan 1992

will be negated by other forces and predictable reactions produced by the overall system of forces. "Common-sense" reform will not work. While indicating the motives which might be harnessed to produce result in educational change, it also shows the difficulty of linking those motives to the points at which systemic interventions might be targeted.

In more detail, the diagram shows:

1. That the narrow educational activities which dominate schools are produced by: (*i*) a series of sociological imperatives (eg, that schools assist in legitimizing the rationing of privilege); (*ii*) inappropriate beliefs about the nature of the changes that are needed in education itself, the management of the educational system, and the management of society; (*iii*) failure to initiate research which would yield useful insights into such things as (a) the nature of competence and how it is to be fostered, and (b) how to manage the educational system to nurture high-level generic competencies; (*iv*) the absence of (a) systematically generated variety in, and choice between, educational programs which have demonstrably different consequences, and (b) information on the consequences of each of these alternatives; (*v*) failure to introduce "parallel organization activity" to produce innovation within schools, and (*vi*) inadequate dissemination of the results of research into the nature, development, and assessment of generic high-level competencies, and, especially, the implications of the values basis of competence.

2. That this narrow educational process has a series of knock-on effects which finally contribute to its own perpetuation. The competencies and beliefs that are nurtured and inculcated in schools reinforce a social order which offers major benefits to "able" people who do what is required of them without questioning that order; it creates endless work which gives meaning to people's lives (but does not enhance the general quality of life);

it creates wealth at the expense of the biosphere, future generations, and the third world; and it protects its citizens from a knowledge of the basis of their wealth. The educational system helps to teach a host of incorrect beliefs which collectively result in nothing being what it is popularly or authoritatively said to be (for example, the educational system itself claims to be about promoting the growth of competence when it in fact mainly operates to engage vast numbers of people in "teaching" and "learning" activities of little educational merit but which ensure that those who are most able and willing to challenge the fraudulent nature of the system are routed to social positions from which they can have little influence, while those who are least able to do anything except secure their own advantage are promoted into influential positions in society). This double-talk makes it extremely difficult to conduct any rational discussion of the changes needed in society. The sociological imperative that schools help to legitimize the rationing of privilege helps to create a demand for, and encourages acceptance of, narrow, invisible, and mislabeled assessments. Those predisposed to acquire these "qualifications" are not inclined to see the need for, or to commission, genuine enquiry-oriented research or notice other talents in their fellows. Teachers who discover the hidden competencies of their "less able" students experience acute distress. The lack of understanding of the nature of competence leads to a failure to underline the need for a variety of value-based educational programs and thus to the perpetuation of narrow educational activity.

That the main motives for change are widespread awareness that there is something seriously wrong with the educational system, and, more specifically, that it fails miserably in its manifest task of identifying, nurturing, recognizing, and utilizing most people's motives and talents. The most commonly proposed solutions to this problem, based as they are on other misunderstandings, are, however, inappropriate. Another motive for change is that there is increasing recognition that we have created a non-sustainable society and that basic change in the way society is run is essential.

4. That there are a number of points at which it should be possible to intervene in the feedback loops to create an upward spiral. These involve: (*i*) promoting wider recognition that one cannot get value for human effort in modern society unless we introduce better means of monitoring and evaluating the long term effects of what we are doing and improve ways of giving effect to information on such effects. This points to the need to change the way we run society, to the need to introduce more, and more appropriate, social research and evaluation activity, and to find ways of holding public servants and politicians accountable for seeking out and acting on information in an innovative way in the long term public interest; (*ii*) introducing the "parallel organization" activities that are required to promote innovation within schools; (*iii*) establishing a greater variety of distinctively different, value-based, educational programs and providing information on the short and long term, personal and social, consequences of each; (*iv*) creating public debate about the forms of supervision—the nature of the democracy—needed to ensure that public servants seek out and act on information in an innovative way in the public interest and, (*v*) disseminating what is already known about the nature, development, and assessment of competence and its implications.

The developments hinted at in the last paragraph will be discussed in Part II of this book.

PART II

MANAGING THE EDUCATIONAL SYSTEM FOR EFFECTIVE EDUCATION

or

CREATING AN INNOVATIVE EDUCATIONAL SYSTEM

CHAPTER 8

THE INTERNAL ORGANIZATION OF THE SYSTEM

To introduce this chapter, what has been said in Part I of this book may be summarized. We have seen that:

(1)   The most important goals in education are heavily value-laden. This gives rise to a host of problems. It means, among other things, that it will be necessary to find ways of handling the difficulties which arise because, although teachers necessarily influence values, they need to do so more explicitly if they are to achieve their main goals, deal with the difficulties involved in assessing value-laden motivational dispositions (especially as part of the certification process), and consider the nature of the information-based public management structures—the forms of bureaucracy and democracy—required if the public is to be offered a choice between programs fostering a wide variety of value-based motivational dispositions.

(2)   The failure of society to come to terms with the value-laden nature of competence makes it difficult for schools to identify individuals' values, interests, and areas of competence. This contributes to the inability of the educational system to achieve its main goals—but it also has serious consequences for society as a whole: It makes for unnecessary frustration and misery among adults, an inability to identify and capitalize upon valuable human resources, and the promotion into influential positions of people lacking the willingness and the ability to tackle broader societal problems.[8.1]

3)   Most teachers are unable to identify their pupils' values, create the developmental environments required to harness those values in such a way that pupils will engage in activities which will lead them to practice and develop high-

level competencies, or to recognize and reward the development of pupils' high-level competencies.

More generally, we have seen that the introduction of a more effective educational system will require change at all levels. Teachers must pay attention to the needs of each individual child, devise a personalized developmental program to harness the child's motives and develop his or her idiosyncratic talents, monitor the effects of such activities, and adapt their activity where necessary. Tools will be needed to help teachers administer these programs, evaluate and assess their outcomes, and to credit pupils and teachers for having developed important competencies. Administrators, working with teachers and researchers, must devise a much wider range of different **types** of educational program, and provide the public with information on the consequences of each. It will be necessary to influence the tests employed at the interface between the school system and society (because it is what is assessed in these tests which primarily determines what happens in schools) and it will be necessary to reduce the societal demand that schools legitimize the rationing of privilege. **Systemic**—multi-pronged—theoretically-based intervention is required. This can only occur if a new management structure is introduced to provide new roles for pupils, teachers, principals, superintendents, politicians, parents, and the public.

Such pervasive change can only be achieved by creating a climate dedicated to innovation. All teachers need to pursue different goals with different pupils, and many of the necessary developments can only be introduced as teachers and administrators exercise professional discretion in dealing with the changing and idiosyncratic requirements of complex situations.

Although change is required in every nook and cranny of the educational system, and will not occur solely as a result of central decree, the establishment of an innovative climate can and should be centrally facilitated. Such a climate can only be achieved by changing (1) the way things are done within the educational system itself, and (2) the interface between the educational system and society.

This chapter will discuss the changes needed in the internal organization of the educational system. Chapter 9 will discuss the changes needed in the interface between that system and society. Chapter 10 will deal with the research and development activity required to help evolve and support the new system.

Essentially, the argument presented here is that putting the translation of the shared educational values identified earlier in this book into practice will *necessitate* following the research-based trail on which we have embarked well beyond even the controversial conclusions upon which we have already stumbled in order to discern its implications for the management of society. It will emerge that, unless this step is taken, other developments will yield few benefits. It is, however, essential to understand that this is a *scientific* step and that the position developed here is reasonably consistent with the available evidence. Further research-based activity is required to clarify alternative positions and assess their adequacy.

An unexpected benefit will be obtained from this journey. It will emerge that the arrangements which are required to translate our educational values into effect are precisely those required to translate crucially important wider social and environmental values into effect.

Before we move on, it is important to briefly review the reasons why "privatization" of the educational system could not provide a solution to the problems which have been identified.

Firstly, even when desired benefits *can* be obtained through the economic marketplace, this is typically a very expensive process. For example, about two thirds of the cost of consumer goods is spent on distribution and advertising. If we spent even one third of what is currently spent on "education" on an effective system of evaluation and development, we would surely have a better educational system than anything which could be achieved through privatization.[8.2] Market management is subject

104

to gross inefficiency. Indeed, the explicit management of the market through taxes, grants, and levies, together with investment in non-market driven R&D (including military R&D), has contributed virtually all the major improvements in efficiency (e.g. in agriculture, communications technology, and transportation) that have been introduced in the past half century.[8.3] The seductive quality of market mythology derives from the way in which it creates large numbers of "high-level" jobs while ostensibly working to increase efficiency by reducing the numbers directly employed in low level jobs, as in the case of insurance discussed in the last chapter.

Because finding a way of tackling the problems of the educational system has centrally to do with finding a way of handling the conflict between its educational and vocational goals on the one hand and the sociological functions it performs in society on the other, it is important to spell out the message of the last paragraph in slightly more detail. It is that:

(1) even in the short term, no society-wide economic benefits derive from market management;

(2) in the longer term the societal economic disbenefits of market management are huge;

(3) some people—those who benefit from the creation of vast numbers of "middle class" jobs—do derive economic benefits from privatization;

(4) privatization and market management contributes in extremely important ways to the cementation and perpetuation of a sociological system which has acquired a life of its own.

Another difficulty with a market solution to the problems of the educational system arises from the fact that what people are buying when they invest in education is not typically an improvement in their competence, but a passport for admission to a protected occupation. The privatization of education—as illustrated by the privately funded cram schools which occupy half the working life of Japanese children—leads to the attainment of economically valuable, but educationally meaningless, credentials. It leads to a narrowing of education and to a focus only on the qualities that are assessed at the point of interface between schools and other institutions, such as colleges and workplaces. Since such assessment is necessarily norm-referenced, there can be no general improvement in schools' ability to deliver even these credentials. Instead, privatization makes for even greater differences between "good" schools and "bad" ones.[8.4] Why should anyone try to improve the schools for those who have "failed" and who will enter low status, powerless, positions? Under these circumstances, *no* school—whether for the future managers of society or the future artisans—can afford to focus on fostering the qualities the pupils will need.[8.5]

As we have seen in the last chapter, the developments most urgently needed in education can take place only if a way can be found to provide parents and pupils with a choice between very different types of programs which cater for a wide variety of needs. In theory, market mechanisms should lead to the provision of such variety. In practice, however, if schools are to offer variety, it will be necessary to change the criteria which are used to assess pupils at the point of interface between schools and society. To influence the assessment procedure, privatized schools would need to band together to fund the necessary—fairly fundamental—research and development. Similar collaboration would be required to evolve the new curriculum specifications that are required and the tools needed to translate them into practice.

There is also the question of how parents and pupils are to influence what happens *in* schools. Because of constraints on geographical mobility and income, most people will always have little effective choice between different types of schools if provision of that variety is left to the marketplace. Some areas will have good schools and others poor ones. Even when there is a choice, schools tend to offer educational *packages*, most of the elements of which fail to meet a particular child's or parent's needs. It follows that, to get what they need, parents and pupils must be able to influence what goes on *within* schools.

Another problem is that some minority groups (most notably the handicapped and the poor) need special provision within education. Unfortunately, in society as it is currently organized, those in greatest need are also those least able to meet the greater financial costs of special provision.

Finally, education is not the sole province of pupils and their parents. The beliefs inculcated in schools, and the competencies they foster (or neglect to foster), have dramatic consequences for society as a whole.

Why, then, apart from being an understandable reaction against uniform and inadequate provision offered by hard-to-influence bureaucrats, are the pressures to privatization so strong? At least seven sociological processes seem to be at work:

(1) As has been the case when other services have been privatized, privatization would create many more high-level, administrative, jobs which would "demand" more "well-educated" employees—preparing brochures, collecting and keeping account of vouchers and payments, and servicing committees.

(2) Because "good" and "poor" schools would become more sharply differentiated, there would be a stronger incentive for pupils to spend more time in the system trying to avoid the fate of the "less able." This would create still more jobs, keep young people off the streets, and, because the goals would have become clearer, make it easier to hold teachers and pupils "accountable" for "success."

(3) It would more strongly favor the sons and daughters of those who could pay more—ie, those already in positions of power.

(4) It would ensure that those who are either (*i*) more anxious and able to obtain promotion by doing whatever other people want them to do regardless of the social and long term consequences of performing that task or

(*ii*) least able or willing to question and analyze the workings of our present system would do "well," are more likely to get promoted. In both these ways a privatized system would be more likely to promote the sort of person our society "needs" to promote the vacuous claims of its manufacturers and service providers and reinforce their claim to having produced them "efficiently" (while in fact doing the opposite).

(5) It would make it easier for those charged with the management of society—public servants and politicians—to lay the blame for the ills of society at the door of the poor. Instead of having to live up to the public's belief that they have appointed politicians and bureaucrats to manage society in the public interest, it would be possible for these public servants to claim that, if only the poor worked hard and made intelligent choices, they would be able to better themselves.

(6) It would reinforce the tendency to blame teachers working in schools serving deprived areas—and not the managers of the social system—for the poor performance of their pupils since, obviously, they would have had the same resources as everyone else but made poorer use of them.

(7) It would shift the locus of responsibility for the problems in education from the leaders and managers of society to those least able to introduce change—teachers, pupils and parents. It would become still less obvious that it is the competence (and therefore the education) of the leaders and managers of our society—and not that of unskilled workers—that is most deficient.

It follows from this discussion that *public* provision is needed to create the necessary choice between educational programs, to collect and disseminate information on their consequences, and to develop the mechanisms, information, and tools required for effective education. Unfortunately, whether one considers education, housing, health, transport, or the environment, these are the very problems the public sector has proved least capable of tackling. Bureaucrats have long neglected the task of identifying social constraints and the means to overcoming them with a view to running systems more effectively. Instead, searching for uniformity and an easy justification for their own positions, they have tended to usurp responsibility for decisions which should have been taken by people lower down in the hierarchy—in this case, by schools and teachers themselves. The problem we face, then, is how to ensure that public servants play an appropriate role in the management of society.

Our focus during the remainder of this book will be on the question of how to create a vibrant and innovative public sector, and how to ensure that public servants (including teachers) act innovatively and in the long term interests of their clients by setting out to influence the various feedback loops shown in Diagram 1 in Chapter 7.

Parallel Organization Activity

The development of an educational system concerned with innovation and improvement, in which people at all levels try to do their jobs *well*, and in which they collaborate in order to influence the wider social forces limiting their actions, will require fundamental change in the way education is managed. It will be necessary to introduce a significant emphasis on what Kanter has termed "parallel organization" activity.[8.6]

According to Kanter—and her conclusions are supported by our own research and that carried out by Spencer—most innovative activity is *not* carried out by a separate cadre of R&D specialists, but by those who undertake the day to day work of the organization.

The main requirements for effective "parallel organization" activity are that:

(1) Time and resources are set aside for activities intended to result in innovation and improvement.

109

(2) People work in a non-hierarchical relationships. Innovation requires fluid networks of *ad hoc* working groups, forming and disbanding as needs change. These groups bring together a wide variety of people, and thereby facilitate the identification, development, and utilization of normally unrecognized talents to create climates of enterprise or innovation (or what Gardner[8.7] has called cultures of intelligence). Whereas novel, potentially risky, ideas tend to be filtered out in hierarchical organizations, flat, non-hierarchical, arrangements bring those with such ideas into direct contact with those capable of releasing resources. The arrangements make it possible for the organization to capitalize on the insights of "coal face" workers instead of relying on "management" or "research" to initiate new developments.

(3) Managers (school principals) and staff recognize the wide range of contributions required to carry out any kind of innovative activity, and assemble teams of people who contribute in very different ways to the exercise.

(4) Managers and other staff identify those best able to undertake effective innovative activity, and channel the necessary resources to them. (Note that people's ability to succeed in such demanding, "risky," and adventurous activity is often unrelated to their ability to produce the formal paper "plans" so cherished by bureaucrats.)

(5) There are opportunities to work with people engaged with similar problems, both within the organization (school) and outside it. Such collaboration generates new ideas and establishes and maintains a network of contacts to provide help and support when difficulties arise. "Cascade" networks of this kind have proved crucial in other fields.[8.8]

110

(6) Staff are encouraged to form "political coalitions" with others outside their own organization (school) in order to find ways of influencing external constraints. In education, these include parental expectations, the sociological functions the educational system performs for society, the expectations of those who currently manage education, and the assessment procedures available.

(7) There is access to R&D laboratories developing the required concepts, understandings, and tools, but in such a way that those concerned (in this case teachers, pupils, and parents) are able to initiate and take part in the research and development process.

Components of a Climate Conducive to Innovation and Improvement

The remainder of this chapter will be devoted to discussing the components of "parallel organization" activity in greater detail, using a framework developed by McClelland and co-workers.[8,9]

A climate conducive to innovation in schools would be one in which teachers' motivational dispositions were developed and released, enabling them to engage in more innovative activity themselves, and allowing them to gain control over social constraints on their classroom behavior. Such an environment would necessitate at least the following:

Concern with clarity

Effective goal achievement requires clarity concerning the goals that are to be achieved, how they are to be reached, how to determine whether they *are* being reached, and how to overcome the barriers to their achievement. However, the "clarity" of an idea does not demand its "clear" formulation in words. Innovatory activity often originates in *feelings*. One might, for

111

instance, become vaguely aware that something is not quite right, or that it might be important to embark on a particular activity. Such feelings lead directly to "experimental interactions with the environment" in which one initiates some activity to see what happens. The results of such activities are also often monitored affectively rather than intellectually. The whole process may lead to an "understanding" which remains unverbalized. Although this process is often non-cognitive, then, there is a sense in which anyone undertaking such activity *is* concerned with clarifying problems, their nature, and potential solutions. It is a lack of such concern which characterizes much of the standardless activity which occupies so much of the time of so many of the pupils in our schools.

In collaborative work, the success of an innovative program of activity demands clear delineation of the roles to be played by everyone concerned.

Explicit emphasis on the importance of innovation

One of the most important prerequisites for innovation and improvement is a belief that it is important to find new ways of thinking about things, better ways of doing things, and new things to do. This is at odds with the belief that everything would be fine if only the government introduced some particular regulation or provided more money. Our research indicates that, by international standards, the UK and the United States have relatively few people who think it is important to do these things. Given that teachers powerfully communicate their own priorities of this sort—and the competencies they use to translate them into effect—to their pupils, it is therefore vitally important that teachers both undertake more activity in this area themselves and explicitly set out to influence students' priorities and competencies in the area by providing the requisite concepts and using literature and case history material to discuss the components of such behavior and illustrate the personal and social consequences. The *Edinburgh Questionnaires* have been developed to help groups such as teachers to collect personal and group data which will enable them to take a look at themselves in a kind of a mirror and ask whether they like the look of what they expect the consequences to be.

Recognition of accomplishment using a differentiated model of competence

As has been mentioned, innovativeness, enterprise, and most forms of intelligence are cultural rather than individual characteristics. Successful innovation requires that one builds on the work of others, and that one's work is itself built upon. A good design for a locomotive is of no use if the materials required to build it are not available, if the track on which it is to run will not be built, and if an appropriate monetary system and a means of collecting fares have not been developed.

An integral feature of any innovative climate is some means of recognizing the contributions of those who are good at initiating action, those who are good at experimenting "intuitively" with the environment, lateral thinkers, people who test ideas and insights, soothers, persuaders, motivators, team builders, grantsmen, publicists, people who examine (and gain control over) external constraints, people who formalize and disseminate understandings built up in the course of "failed" projects (so that it ceases to be true that such projects are failures), and people able to sift information for forward-looking, *potentially* useful, ideas.

The establishment of such a climate depends on general recognition that people possess very different talents and on the development of support systems which assist those who are doing different things in carrying out those activities. People using their most important abilities to good effect should not be castigated for neglecting other aspects of their work.

It is important to note that innovative activity often does not lead to tangible results. Such difficult, demanding, and frustrating activity is frequently fruitless. No one should be considered only as good as the success of their latest venture. Of much greater importance are the understandings and competencies developed over a long period of time.

This discussion underlines the need for a mechanism whereby all contributions and accomplishments, however intangible, can be recognized and credited. Hence the importance of the descriptive statements concerning competence which emerge from the network-based observations and informal assessments form part of "parallel organization" activity. However, there is a clear need to formalize such knowledge by developing the means to assess and report high-level competencies as part of the staff-appraisal process. Thereafter, systematic procedures are needed for the identification, development and utilization of previously unrecognized competencies. Exactly such a system has been developed by Adams and Burgess.[8.10] Teachers and head teachers keep a record of activities they consider important, including accounts of their hopes, aspirations, and disappointments. This enables them to assess their own accomplishments and make plans for the future. The discussion of such accounts among colleagues leads to a mutual understanding of each others' motives, values, hopes, and competencies. Colleagues, superiors, and subordinates become better able to support, encourage, and capitalize upon, each others' talents. Subordinates are able to *participate* in the "managerial" process of setting organizational and individual goals, receiving recognition for their contributions *in terms which are personally important to them.*

An emphasis on staff development and the creation of developmental environments

Innovation in schools requires a wide variety of people to perform very different functions. It follows that the emphasis in staff assessment should be on guidance, placement, and development rather than selection. This emphasis on staff development is reinforced by the fact that these divergent, but important, competencies are typically best developed on the job. Taken together, these observations suggest that out-of-school teacher training should largely be abandoned.

In fact, the establishment of a climate of innovation within the educational system requires the creation of *developmental environments* from which *everyone*—principals, teachers, and pupils alike—will benefit. Just as pupils need opportunities to practice and develop high-level competencies, staff need opportunities to participate in innovative activity, and thus become familiar with the cyclical learning processes required for successful innovation. Instead of depending on centralized direction, they need to learn how to engage in the step-wise process of trial, monitoring, "reflection," and improvement.

Just as school staff need to refrain from expecting their superiors to provide solutions to their problems, so they must refrain from blaming their colleagues when things go wrong. Activities that are easily denigrated as "failures" need to be regarded as opportunities to learn more about the nature of the problem and the adequacy of the strategies to be used to solve them. School staff also need experience in gaining control over external forces, including those arising from parents and the range of tests that are available, and come to view such activities as crucial parts *of their jobs*. They need opportunities to participate in the management of their schools, not by serving on committees, but through the active performance of managerial roles—setting goals, motivating people to work together effectively, and dealing with those inclined to sabotage the process. They need to take more responsibility for their own development and set up networks of contacts which help them to keep abreast of developments in their own specialist area.[8.11]

Support

It is essential, in any innovative environment, that colleagues offer each other help and support when difficulties are encountered. Any criticism offered must be constructive rather than destructive, emphasizing the worthwhile aspects of the task accomplished rather than its failures. New ideas floated among a group of colleagues should be examined for their innovatory potential rather than their limitations and practical problems.

Participation in management

Principals are formally appointed as school managers. However, we have already seen that hierarchical management structures are not appropriate to all the tasks which need to be undertaken in modern society. At one time it seemed as if the relationships to be established between managers and their staff would be subsumed within the concept of "democratic management," with its emphasis on delegation of responsibility. However, Schon[8.12] has pointed to the need to think about organizations in a more differentiated way and to make room for people performing a range of functions: inter-organizational gofers, fixers, visionaries, "young turks" (who challenge received views), advocates, brokers, maneuverers, etc. More recently, Kanter has questioned the whole notion of innovative activity within hierarchical structures which do not provide for "parallel organization activity." The widespread confusion created by equating accountability hierarchies with pay hierarchies has been underlined by Jaques.[8.13]

Of great importance in this context are the expectations we have of public servants, including teachers. We will examine these expectations in greater detail in the next chapter, but it is necessary to anticipate that discussion here to the extent that it is important to recognize that ways must be found to hold managers (head teachers and principals) accountable for releasing the energy, enthusiasm, and know-how of their subordinates (in this case teachers). At the same time, it will be necessary to find ways of holding subordinates accountable for individual innovative activity. A few elected representatives at the top of a bureaucratic hierarchy simply cannot deal with the quantity of information involved. To a considerable extent, then, it is the manager's job to monitor the performance of subordinates as a basis for important decisions concerning their placement and development.[8.14] The exercise of such managerial discretion cannot be delegated to committees, or replaced by "democratic" decision-making among staff. Managerial performance must therefore be evaluated against such criteria as whether those concerned are able to carry out these kinds of activity effectively.[8.15]

A manager's role in any organization involves making discretionary judgments about which activities are to be carried out. This involves judging the character of subordinates in order to decide to whom to channel resources; it involves deciding which potentially valuable (but as yet untried and untested) new developments should be initiated; it involves thinking about the talents of subordinates and how to place, develop, and capitalize upon them; it involves creating a developmental and innovative environment; it involves opening doors for energetic and innovative subordinates so that they can undertake the activities they are strongly motivated to carry out; and it involves deciding how best to work with other managers to gain control over external constraints on what can be done within the organization.

Participation in the management process is designed to ensure that all concerned understand what is to be done and how it is to be done, to foster commitment to the organization and new developments, to help clarify the variety of different roles required, and to encourage effective performance of those roles.[8.16] But it can also play an important part in staff development by enabling subordinates to participate in their managers' thought processes, their prioritizing, their anticipation of future difficulties and invention of ways round them, their establishment of "political coalitions" to gain control over forces from outside their organizations, their feelings of doubt and the way in which they take initial soundings and grow in confidence, and other features of personal and managerial competence.[8.17]

The term "delegation of responsibility" is confusing and misleading. It implies that managers are to hand over some part of their job. Instead, jobs need to be *defined* to include responsibility for such things as taking initiative, exercising judgment and discretion, initiating action based on feelings, monitoring developments with a view to improvement, etc. Looked at in this way, the person concerned already *has* responsibility for trying to invent better ways of meeting clients' needs. No one should have to spend a great deal of time trying to justify prospective courses of action to those without first-hand knowledge of a problem, or a knowledge of the personal resources which can be brought to bear to invent ways of overcoming unexpected difficulties.

Changes in job definitions of teachers and principals

At present, teachers, and public servants generally, are not expected to engage in spontaneous innovative activity. Neither is it seen as part of their role to find better ways of meeting their clients' needs or to influence the social constraints which prevent them doing so. Instead, they are looked upon as functionaries who are expected to do the bidding of elected representatives.

If teachers are to concern themselves more with the needs of their pupils than with the directives of elected representatives, they must be held accountable for making good, discretionary, forward-looking decisions in their pupils' interests instead of for following the directives of their superiors. They must be held accountable for recognizing their pupils' individual motivational dispositions and talents, and for creating personalized developmental programs designed to nurture these talents. They must be held accountable for collaborating with others in order to influence external constraints and for initiating and engaging in a public debate concerning the goals of education and how they are to be achieved. They must, in fact, be held accountable for carrying out all those activities which constitute innovative action in the public interest.[8.18]

In a similar vein, the principals' job is to create a climate of enthusiasm, dedication, high standards, and concern with innovation. This requires them to gain control over external constraints and to form political[8.19] coalitions for the purpose. It requires them to identify those able to make good use of resources, and to allocate resources and support personnel accordingly. It requires them to identify and harness the different talents possessed by different teachers, and to ensure that teachers get recognition for their activities. It requires them to assemble teams of people

118

capable of contributing very different things to a program of innovation, and to translate conflicts in individual priorities into useful activity.[8.20]

Systematic monitoring and review activities

Our research has revealed an urgent need for more regular and systematic clarification within schools of educational goals, assessment of whether they are being achieved, if not why not, and what can be done about it. There is, at present, little activity of this kind. Any monitoring which takes place tends to be linked to staff selection rather than staff development, and is therefore threatening rather than supportive. We have also noted a great deal of skepticism concerning the value of systematic monitoring activity. This seems to derive from two sources. First, it is rightly suspected that any formal measures of goal achievement which might be introduced would not reflect the most important goals of education because these are "intangible and difficult to measure." The introduction of a narrow range of measures would yield misleading results and lead to a concentration on easily assessed goals and the neglect of more important ones.[8.21] Second, it's commonplace that the results of evaluation exercises tend to disappear into the files of some external agency without having any effect on educational programs.[8.22]

More systematic activity requires both informal and formal monitoring.

Informal monitoring

Kanter's work shows that informal discussion between those involved in innovative activity *does* lead to progress. In an educational setting, more informal meetings between staff (in the course of parallel-organization activity) could be extremely useful if the discussion focused on goals, the means to achieving them, and barriers to their achievement.

It is important to avoid citing the elusiveness of important educational goals as an excuse for failing to monitor progress toward them: failure to introduce appropriate monitoring arrange-

119

ments leads to a neglect of **all** standards. Any attempt to develop ways of measuring, or indexing, important but intangible outcomes and the ways in which they are being achieved leads to greater clarity concerning goals, their achievement, and their assessment.

In any case, many goals are not so intangible as is often claimed. This is usefully illustrated by an example from one of our own projects.

In seeking to discover whether primary school teachers utilized out-of-school visits in ways which would foster high-level competencies in their pupils, we examined displays produced by schools for inclusion in an exhibition of work arising from a zoo visit. Most of the exhibits consisted of pictures of animals, accompanied by statements about conservation or the animals depicted. There was little evidence that the visits had been used to develop the pupils' powers of observation, their ability to form an understanding of ecological processes, the influence of economics in such processes, or the pupils' understanding of their own role in this cycle. Similarly, our observations of the murals which children and their teachers had constructed in schools revealed little evidence of original observation, collaborative work, leadership, or the use of layout to communicate an unwritten message. It appeared that the teachers' focus had been almost exclusively on low-level language skills, craft work, and book-reference skills. Clearly, the work "behind" the displays and murals involved much closed questioning and an emphasis on what are so often called "academic" skills—low-level memorization, which involves no judgment, analysis, synthesis, or critical thinking.[8.23]

These examples illustrate that an attempt to obtain evidence concerning the attainment of educational goals leads to improved understanding, both of the goals to be achieved and the means to their achievement.

Formal evaluation

Two kinds of formal evaluation activity need to be considered: Outcome Focused and Intervening-Process Focused evaluation.

Outcome focused evaluation. Formal evaluation procedures are most useful when an attempt is being made to reach clear goals. In education it is difficult to assess progress toward many important goals, and the qualities to be nurtured vary greatly from pupil to pupil. If this type of evaluation is not to direct attention away from the most important goals, it is essential that it be broadly based and cover *all* important outcomes.[8.24]

Intervening-process focused evaluation. This concerns the *likelihood* that certain activities will lead to desired outcomes. Classroom activity can be indexed using sophisticated "classroom climate"[8.25] schedules focusing on high-level educational processes. This can be done by asking pupils about such things as the values of fellow pupils and teachers, the kinds of activities which are encouraged and rewarded, whether they think it important to attempt new things, and what they think would be the consequences of such attempts. Walberg and Howard[8.26] (and many others in the industrial sector) have shown that information collected using such measures can be used to create more productive and developmental environments. The classroom environment data collected by Howard were fed to a series of groups made up of parents, teachers, and administrators. They were asked whether they liked what they saw, what its consequences were likely to be, and what could be done to improve the situation. Repeat assessments were made to see whether the suggested changes had had the desired effect. Note that what the bureaucracy was doing was providing measures and then feeding information outward to the public rather than upward through a bureaucratic hierarchy. Note also the use of a multi-interest external group to give teeth to the information collected.

These observations suggest that the formal review process is less important than the understandings and procedures accompanying it. To be functional, those understandings and procedures must recognize the value of pursuing hunches. The real objectives and purpose of an activity often only emerge through monitoring the results of "experimental" behavior initiated on the basis of feelings. Review processes must acknowledge the importance of supportive *discussion* geared to the generation of enthusiasm and understanding, rather than gaining an accurate measure of the "quality" of previous performance. It is the cyclical improvement in depth of understanding which results in innovation— one cannot plan an adventure into the unknown with any precision. Review processes to support and stimulate innovation must be flexible and encourage those concerned to capitalize on "chance" discoveries, learn from "mistakes," and follow up unanticipated leads. Reassurance and help is often needed to overcome the fears and anxieties associated with the exploration of unknown territory.

In concluding this section, it is important to note that these procedures, while forming a necessary part of an effective educational system, have an even more important role to play: they expose pupils to the procedures required to create an innovative society.

Procedures for handling conflict

In creating a climate which supports innovation, explicit steps need to be taken to ensure that differences of opinion come out into the open and are dealt with. Nothing undermines the effectiveness of an organization more than a tendency on the part of its employees to acquiesce when decisions are being made but then to engage in activities which undermine those decisions.

What is needed is shared recognition that it is important to pay attention to differences of opinion, mull them over, and make their implications explicit. Differences of opinion do not have to be interpreted as signs of personal animosity. Indeed, they should be regarded as positive tensions offering springboards to action. It is very important to avoid the tendency to merely acknowledge and accept them by such mechanisms as attributing them to "personality clashes." This merely absolves those concerned from responsibility for thinking about the *cause* of the problem.

Encouragement to work outside the school to identify and tackle wider constraints

Schools do not exist in isolation. Teachers' activities are markedly affected by the expectations of pupils, parents, Directors of Education, members of advisory services, and the principals of other schools (particularly those to which graduates of their school will proceed). More fundamentally, perhaps, teachers' actions are controlled by the role played by schools in the process of social selection and placement. These social forces are manifested in the demands made on schools by parents, and in the coercive power of the assessment system. Pupils appreciate the dilemmas associated with spending time on activities which foster high-level competencies if this leads to lower subject grades.

In the past, even the role of school principal has not been considered to include such things as engaging in public debate concerning the goals of education and the means to their achievement. However, so much activity is required outside schools that not only principals, but the entire school staff, need to become involved.

But this is not the only reason for emphasizing the need to encourage more teachers to become involved in out-of-school activities. It is easiest to make some of the other reasons clear by an example. Teachers seldom know how to deal with a group of parents demanding change, particularly when different parents demand incompatible changes. They tend not to define such situations as problems which are capable of analysis and solution. Instead they tend to avoid creating situations which would lead them to have to deal with them. It is too much to expect most teachers to solve such problems on their own. We need to ensure that teachers can, through "parallel organization" activity, initiate

123

the research needed to clarify such problems and participate in the activities required to tackle them.

The links between the educational system and the "outside world" have been summarized in Diagram 1 at the end of Chapter 7. That diagram reveals the multiple interacting forces which need to be influenced, the motives which can be harnessed to influence them, and the points at which it would be possible to intervene. The task now is to find ways of doing so.[8.27]

External support

Those engaged in innovative activity cannot expect to meet with the approval of everyone they encounter. If they are not to be discouraged, it is essential that innovators have a network of contacts outside their own organization to provide support, ideas, and encouragement.

Rogers'[8.28] research has shown that high-level innovators establish cosmopolitan networks of contacts which allow them access to developing intellectual ideas. However, others have networks which enable them to observe the work, and adopt the practices, of contacts at a similar level in the hierarchy of innovation. If people are required to review the work of those too far ahead in their field, they tend to dismiss the work as inappropriate to their own situation, citing differences in resources, clientele, etc. A facilitative "cascade" structure is required in education, and the need is not satisfied by an imposed cascade structure involving training which takes no account of the person's present position and competencies, or external constraints.

An appropriate concept of risk

Suggestions as to how public provision might be improved are often met with the view that nothing can be done because the suggestion has not been tried, tested, and shown to work—"One cannot take risks with public money." The truth behind such assertions is that public servants are averse to taking responsibility for risky activities suggested by those below them in the bureaucracy or outsiders. Given what has been said above concerning the role of public servants in the management of modern society, such abdication of responsibility cannot be allowed to continue. However, public servants *do* need opportunities to develop the competencies required to undertake adventurous activities, just as the public need to develop more appropriate standards and criteria against which to evaluate the activities of public servants.

In order to reap the benefits of innovation, a reasonable degree of failure must be anticipated. There must be greater tolerance of false starts coupled with an enhanced capacity to learn from adventures that have "failed" and subsequently capitalize on what has been learned. The risk to be taken is not a gambler's risk, but simply that involved in a speculative attempt to find a way of ameliorating a problem or effect important change. It should always be possible to learn enough from an adventure to justify having undertaken it. However, if enhanced understanding is to be a sufficient justification for having embarked upon adventurous activity, it will be necessary to have some formal mechanism to crystallize and disseminate what has been learned. This will often require those concerned to employ researchers with particular skills in this area and then encourage them, not merely to write articles, but also to disseminate—and revise—what has been learned through the network-based management structures which were hinted at above and which will be described more fully in the next chapter.

The conclusion to which this discussion points is that a climate which is conducive to innovation must, while tolerating failure and resisting the temptation to insist that one be certain that any particular course of action will succeed before embarking on it, ensure that those concerned have the competencies and expectations, and access to the support structures, required to ensure that something worthwhile emerges from virtually any activity initiated. All of these are sadly lacking in the educational system at present.

Summary

In this chapter we have discussed the changes needed to create a climate of innovation within the educational system. There is a need to allocate time for, and create appropriate structures to carry out, what Kanter has called "parallel organization activities." These require "flat," non-hierarchical, arrangements which allow information to flow freely between people at different levels in a bureaucratic structure and enable resources to reach innovative individuals. Such activities also require the establishment of networks of contacts within schools and between schools and outside organizations.

More generally, we have discussed those dimensions of organizational climate which require attention if innovation is to be promoted. New job descriptions for principals, teachers, and administrators are called for. It will be necessary to increase teachers' involvement in the management of their schools, and to evolve new concepts of management. Developmental environments must be created for teachers within schools, and they should also be encouraged to spend more time *outside* their schools attempting to gain control over the social constraints which currently prevent them pursuing educational goals effectively within their classrooms. Most important of all, it will be necessary to find ways of giving all concerned credit for engaging in such difficult and demanding activities. Adams and Burgess have developed and tested a mechanism for promoting the flow of information between different levels in a hierarchy, encouraging recognition of neglected concerns and competencies, providing a support structure, and offering recognition for the outcomes. Their work shows that it is *not* necessary to wait for legislation and sociological change before anything can be done: It is *now* possible for teachers to act in a more professional way to gain more control over their destinies and do their jobs more effectively.

A *School Improvement Kit,* designed to help teachers and school systems take stock of, and improve, their climates for innovation, is in preparation.

CHAPTER 9

THE ROLE AND FUNCTION OF PUBLIC SECTOR BUREAUCRACY AND ITS INTERFACE WITH THE PUBLIC

In Chapter 7 we saw that if we are to have an effective educational system, the role played by public servants, including teachers and administrators, will have to change dramatically. They need to undertake a range of thus far unfamiliar activities, exercise a variety of new high-level competencies, and have their performance evaluated against such criteria as their ability to make good discretionary judgments and initiate forward-looking action in the public interest.

More specifically, we saw that in order to solve the problems which arise from the value-laden nature of competence, it will be necessary to (a) develop, experiment with, provide, and evaluate, a much greater variety of different types of educational programs; (b) collect and disseminate—directly to the public—both (*i*) information on the personal and social consequences of each of the options, and (*ii*) evidence that each is of high quality; and (c) evolve ways whereby the public can much more easily influence the nature and quality of provision.

In Chapter 8 we concluded that some of these changes could be achieved by introducing a staff appraisal system to recognize and reward the exercise of high-level competencies by teachers and administrators.

In this chapter it will be argued that others could be achieved by evolving forms of "participative democracy" which would enable the public to play a more direct role in the management of society.

The part played by the public service in the management of modern society is too great and diverse to be adequately monitored by small groups of elected representatives. The material reviewed in this book provides conspicuous evidence of the inability of centralized government and traditional forms of bureaucracy to manage even one area of public provision effectively. Similar evidence could have been produced for many other domains: health care, agriculture, defense, the environment, the biosphere, and the economy itself.[9.1] Changes are needed in the *processes* employed to arrive at information-based decisions and the steps subsequently taken to manage, monitor, and improve the developments that are introduced.

This chapter will discuss the possible nature of these arrangements.

Network-based Supervisory Structures

A more transparent, "decentralized," bureaucratic and representative structure is required to: (a) hold public servants accountable for such things as making good discretionary judgments concerning activities which are likely to be in the long-term public interest; (b) ensure that key information is collected and fed outward to the public (instead of upward through a bureaucratic hierarchy); (c) ensure that action is taken on the results, and (d) ensure that feedback concerning the adequacy of the variety provided and the general direction of activity is obtained and used.

Such a structure might be provided by the fluid networks of monitoring groups discussed in more detail by Toffler,[9.2] Schon,[9.3] Ferguson,[9.4] and Raven,[9.5] and, in some senses, actually operationalized by Howard.[9.6]

In the case of education, we might envisage a structure involving groups of people monitoring the work of individual teachers in their classrooms, groups monitoring the work of schools, clusters of schools, provision in an area, national and international policy, groups examining the work of local and national administrators and administration systems, and groups monitoring the interface between the educational system and society.

The necessity for a *network* of groups can be illustrated by taking an example. Teachers need to assume more responsibility for the innovative action they take as individuals. But to take effective action as individuals, they need to take account of the activities of teachers in the same and other schools and national and international developments. They need assistance in dealing with problems, in clarifying and initiating the coordinated action required to tackle the educational and social problems lying behind everyday difficulties in the classroom, and in making contact with other people trying to tackle related problems. It follows that, since all of these considerations need to be taken into account when evaluating the work of an individual teacher, all this information must, in some sense, be known to the monitoring network.

The groups in a network should have changing, diverse, and overlapping, memberships. They might involve parents, other citizens, a range of staff, researchers, members of other communities, members of central planning organizations, and the media. Overlapping membership encourages the flow of information between different people and different levels in the system.

Howard[9.7] has already instigated activity of this kind. His groups, made up of parents, teachers, pupils, administrators and researchers, were set up to monitor and review the work of schools and individual teachers over an extended period of time. The groups were supplied with information collected using professionally developed questionnaires designed to review educational goals and the barriers to their achievement, and to document activities in individual classrooms. Repeated assessment showed whether the classroom climates had changed as a result of suggested interventions and whether the wider goals of education were being achieved more effectively. The process led to more effective schooling, and to an improvement in the understanding of educational issues on everyone's part.

A great deal remains to be done to determine how such groups should be composed, how their memberships should be decided, how much weight should be attached to different peoples' opinions, how their work should be monitored, and what procedures should be introduced to ensure that they disband when they have outlived their usefulness. However, the solutions to these problems can only be determined through monitored experimentation.[9.8]

It is important that the direct contact between members of such groups be supplemented by effective media coverage of the issues. Those involved need to know what is emerging from research. Computer-based networks are also required to allow contact between like-minded individuals in other parts of the world.

The participants in the groups must be able to initiate the process of information-collection *and* contribute to the definition of problems to be investigated and tackled. We might envisage a media-based debate, with a guaranteed right to contribute and be heard, and assurance that assistance will be available to help people collect the data needed to substantiate their viewpoints. The debate must be linked to voting procedures, but the votes which are to count on any particular issue will in many cases need to be in some way limited to those with an interest in that topic. However, the results of such referenda should not bind policy-making groups. Democracy is more about catering for variety, and allowing consensus to emerge, than establishing majority decisions binding on all. The pattern of votes should be looked upon as one source of information among many to be taken into account by public servants in the decision-making process—and, as we have seen, those public servants should themselves be held accountable to a similar network of monitoring groups for the quality of their discretionary judgment as to what is in the long-term public interest as a whole and the groups of which it is composed.

Researchers have a responsibility to generate the information needed to assess the effectiveness of provision, identify the barriers preventing the achievement of educational goals, clarify the curriculum processes required to reach those goals, study the effectiveness of present administrative arrangements and develop better ones, and develop any tools required for these purposes. Encouraging researchers to participate in the network management structure is one way of helping to ensure that more relevant information is collected for the purpose of formal evaluation. Their involvement is also desirable in that it brings into the decision-making process people who, because of their contact with ideas, the public, the problems, and potential methods of tackling them, are more likely than others to envisage radically new formulations of objectives, problems, and lines of development.

Innovative ideas tend to emerge from networks of individuals who are in touch with each other but somewhat isolated in their own communities.[9.9] The members of these groups are distinguished by their inclination to innovate, an interest in ideas, and a feel for the process of innovation—for experimentation and continuous revision. They also tend to have the time and financial resources required to do new things. They have scope to "take risks" in the knowledge that an error would not be too damaging. Ideas of this kind tend to derive less from managers, who have little contact with the problems themselves or with others working on related problems. Once ideas have been tested and made useful through pilot experiments,[9.10] they tend to be disseminated through the kind of "cascade" system described in the last chapter rather than through the media. People tend to adopt new practices after having seen them working effectively for others in similar conditions. Laggards are brought along by financial and other constraints. Invention is the mother of necessity, not vice versa.

The main influence of this network-based supervisory structure would not derive from its power to hire and fire individual members of staff. Rather, it would stem from its capacity to provide teachers and bureaucrats with a wealth of positive ideas on how to improve their performance, and allow them access to those best able to help them do whatever is necessary. It would help public servants to tap their client's often considerable, if generally neglected, expertise on the issues. However, perhaps the two most important benefits of the process would be (1) the exposure of public servants' activities to the public gaze—a strong incentive for people to act in the public interest, and (2) its ability to provide the public with the information they need to take informed decisions about their own lives and those of their children.

Changes in the Role of Elected Representatives

If such a network of monitoring groups were introduced, responsibility for monitoring the work of the public service would be devolved from central government, but in a very different way to that envisaged in the currently fashionable notion of devolution to assemblies of locally elected representatives. This procedure results in channeling so many decisions through such small numbers of people that those concerned cannot possibly be well informed about more than a fraction of them. A network-based structure implies a participative, as distinct from representative, democracy. The effective operation of such a structure would depend on everyone's faith in the competence of their fellow citizens to make sensible decisions about issues affecting themselves. It is worth noting, however, that such faith would be more justified than faith in representatives elected to multi-purpose assemblies.

The role of the public service will become more, not less, important in any new scheme of things. To it will fall the task of initiating and carrying out the research and evaluation activities required to monitor the effectiveness of public provision. To it will fall the task of clarifying the range of educational programs required, and of disseminating information about the personal and social, short and long-term, consequences of each. Given the crucial importance of all this information, new mechanisms are required, not only to supervise the public service, but also to influence the nature of the information collected, its presentation and discussion, and the considerations taken into account when decisions are made.[9.11]

It should not be concluded from this discussion that there is no role for representative decision-taking bodies. Such bodies must bring into being the international structures needed to manage the global economic arrangements (on which the educational system is so dependent) in the public interest. To such bodies will fall the task of promoting public debate and monitoring the workings of institutional arrangements, including both "parallel organization" activity and the network-based monitoring structures discussed here. It will also be part of their role to make collective decisions, dismissing ideas which benefit individuals rather than society generally.[9.12]

Attention does, however, need to be paid to the way in which members of representative assemblies are chosen. Emery[9.13] has shown that it would be better to do this by sortition—random selection from the group concerned—than by election. Elected representatives tend to have very different concerns, interests, and priorities from the electorate they claim to represent.

It is frequently claimed that a serious difficulty with the above scenario is that "there must be an authority to dismiss incompetent workers." It is felt insufficient to expose the work of incompetent people to the public gaze, and to institute better staff guidance, placement, and development procedures. This claim has a somewhat hollow ring given the evidence that our current hierarchical supervisory structures are typically unable to do anything when faced with incompetent teachers, doctors, and public servants—or even extremely destructive elected politicians. In fact, as Day and Klein[9.14] have observed, public service professionals are generally able to evade *any* form of accountability by arguing that the issues involved are so complex that they can only be understood by fellow professionals. Such views are seriously challenged by the data presented in this book and by public opinion. But the favored remedies for education—centralized prescription of curriculum and testing, tough staff ap-

133

praisal, and devolution of "control" to schools—have been discounted earlier in this book.

It is also claimed that the arrangements envisaged in this and the previous chapter are unrealistic. Critics cite the "top-heaviness" of the proposed system of management, and claim that the public would be loath to devote the necessary time to participation in societal management—however socially beneficial that might actually be— if it would reduce the time available for acquisition of personal wealth.

However, personal wealth will be of little use in a world overwhelmed by the collective effect of ecological and economic catastrophe, and in any case, participation in the management of activities contributing to the quality of life is, in itself, a wealth-creating activity meriting remuneration.

The way forward will involve wider recognition that most wealth in modern society resides in the public domain. The supervision of such things as community support, urban reconstruction, agricultural policy, crime prevention, the management of the economy, and environmental protection, is a wealth-creating activity which people should *not* be expected to undertake without reward.

Much of the discussion in this chapter has been speculative and short of concrete examples. It has been based on research into the nature of competence and the barriers to effective education. It might, perhaps, be possible to reinforce the conclusions we have drawn by undertaking comparative study of the workings of different local government structures, and of the management structures in different countries such as Japan, Germany, Norway and the UK. Once again, therefore, we see that the attempt to solve an applied problem leads directly to a major agenda for fundamental research—for the problem is not to apply existing concepts to the analysis of different societies but to engage in that kind of research which will surface embedded assumptions and incipient movements toward new ways of doing things. Many of these are not articulated by the members of the societies concerned and have to be surfaced through programs of comparative interviewing which are explicitly set up on the understanding that the researcher does not know what questions to ask and is indeed struggling to become clearer about what those questions might be.

Summary

We began this chapter by identifying one of the major problems of modern society as the need to find ways of getting public servants to seek out and act on information in an innovatory way in the public interest. Current bureaucratic and representative structures have proved inadequate to this task. We concluded that exposing the activities of public servants to the public gaze would encourage them to act in a more innovative and responsible fashion. To do this, it would be necessary to introduce network-based structures which would better enable the public to oversee the work of its servants. The role of the public service itself needs to focus more on the promotion of innovation.

In the realm of education, public servants need to generate a range of alternative programs between which the public can be invited to choose, to collect information on the personal and social consequences of each, and to feed that information outward to the public rather than upward through a bureaucratic hierarchy to elected representatives who supposedly make decisions about the programs that are best for everybody.

These changes in our forms of democracy and bureaucracy would complement the changes in the internal functioning of the educational system which were suggested in the last chapter.

Yet, although there is indeed an urgent need for change in the nature of democracy, we do not have to wait for centrally decreed change before *any* progress can be made. Networks of monitoring groups can be established through local initiatives. The work of Adams and Burgess in the UK, and Howard in the US, indicates the possibility of introducing aspects of an innovative climate which are followed, rather than preceded, by changes in management procedures. The adoption of such procedures leads to an improved flow of information between different levels in a bureaucracy, to the establishment of support networks, to the recognition and reward of attempts to seek out and act on information in an innovative way in the public interest, and to the creation of networks to monitor and support the work of individuals.

CHAPTER 10

THE ORGANIZATION AND FACILITATION OF RESEARCH

By way of introduction to this chapter, attention may be drawn to some features of the research on which this book has been based. Much of this research did not conform to widely accepted beliefs about how research should be initiated and funded. It was generally research which involved adventures into the unknown. Several of the enquiries were initiated on the basis of feelings and impressions rather than formal hypotheses. Much of the research had its origin in sensed problems rather than the "research literature." The logical connections which gave meaning to the data (or which provided a "theoretical framework" for collecting or interpreting it) were often made retrospectively. The true significance of the data could often only be discerned if one drew debatable conclusions about underlying structures and processes which go well beyond what could be "proved" by specific data sets.[10.1]

Such research could not have been conducted according to conventional ideas concerning the initiation, funding, execution and evaluation of research.[10.2] The same is likely to be true of the research needed to overcome the problems identified in this book.

The Role of Colleges, Universities, and Research Institutes

In the course of this book we have seen that common sense and established good practice are *not* an adequate basis on which to build a program for remedying the conspicuous problems of the educational system. The causes of these problems are deep-seated and often rooted in causes far removed from their symptoms. They have major value-laden and political components which are often difficult to address in the face of widely held beliefs concerning the workings of society. But the most important points to be noted here are, first, that it has only been possible to uncover many of the causes of otherwise conspicuous problems through research, and, second, that—because of their deep-seated causes—the problems will only be solved through further research-based development activity.

Although colleges and universities have a major role to play in carrying out such research, collecting the information and developing the understandings and tools required to solve the problems facing the educational system are difficult and adventurous activities which are not easily reconciled with the kind of research which has come to characterize university-based social science research over the past 40 years. This has tended to be of an unadventurous, non-controversial, literature-driven (rather than problem-driven), "disciplinary," nature and has often been more concerned with securing the promotion of those concerned than with advancing understanding or solving problems.[10.3] To tackle the problems, we need a wide variety of full-time researchers and institutional arrangements which will enable them to contribute in different ways to team-based applied research with fundamental components which aim to find ways of tackling the conspicuous problems of the educational system in a limited period of time. To help discern the arrangements that are needed, we will first review the range of research that is required in slightly more detail.

The Range of Research Needed

We have seen a need for research to:

- document the personal and societal, short and long-term, consequences of alternative educational programs.

- develop the tools required to monitor the quality of such diverse programs.

- develop a better conceptual framework for thinking about competence, how its varieties and components are to be nurtured, and how its varieties and components are to be assessed.

- develop the tools needed to help bureaucrats administer the necessary variety of educational programs.

- develop the tools which teachers need to help them think about the motives, talents, and latent competencies of their pupils, design individualized educational programs to tap those motives and nurture those talents, and assess the outcomes.[10.4]

- develop a framework for appraising principals, so that they can get credit for creating school environments which release and utilize the talents of classroom teachers.

- develop means of assessing the work of public service administrators so that they can get credit for initiating the collection of forward-looking information, their ability to use such information as is available to make good discretionary judgments about what is in the best long-term interests of society, and their ability to translate those decisions into effect and monitor the results in such a way as to improve the policies which have been implemented.

- clarify the competencies required by head teachers and public servants and the ways in which they can be encouraged to develop and display the desired qualities.

- clarify the links between educational policy on the one hand and policy in other areas (eg, differential incomes and employment policy) on the other and the steps which need to be taken to influence these wider processes.

However, the research which is most urgently needed does not lie at the level of such specific detail. It has to do with the management of society itself. Such research might take the form of experimental action programs designed to test and refine the insights of the last two chapters, or it might investigate the assumptions embedded in the organization of different societies. The research would be designed, not to test previously formulated hypotheses, but to formulate questions which ought to be asked.

The purpose of this chapter is to discuss the institutional arrangements and expectations required to undertake the full range of research required to solve the problems of education.

The Nature and Organization of Research

Fundamental research of the kind discussed above can only be carried out in the context of action. One cannot, for example, develop valid measures of high-level competencies without changing classroom processes so that those competencies are developed and displayed. But to change classroom processes it is necessary to have some means of identifying the important outcomes as part of the certification and placement process. And one cannot change either of these except in the context of new relationships between teachers and schools on the one hand and examination boards, test agencies, local and national employers, and parents and politicians on the other. In other words, one cannot expect to make much progress without careful systems analysis and systemic intervention to prevent parts of the system nullifying the effects of specific interventions.[10.5]

Good research is adventurous, inventive, creative, and pays little respect to "disciplinary" boundaries. Our work on educational objectives and competence, for example, led us to enquire into the nature of modern societies and the political and institutional arrangements required for their effective management.

Improved understanding often stems from public debate about concepts, ways of thinking about things, and the *implications* of data. Many of the insights shared in this book arose through the discussion of conference papers and published articles which now appear to contain naive, sometimes completely incorrect, interpretations of incomplete data. Scientists must be prepared and expected to admit the possibility that they may be wrong in order to clear the way for productive debate. It is vital to distinguish between the outcomes expected from the scientific *process* and those to be expected from the work of an *individual scientist*. The scientific process leads to "truth" and indisputability: yet the demand that the work of an individual be beyond dispute starves the process of much-needed data and insights.

We might draw a number of conclusions from these observations. First, we need more research teams to study "the same" topic from different perspectives. For example, the view of competence, its development and assessment presented in this book is not the only one imaginable, and may well prove to be misguided. Bureaucratic claims that there is no need for a given project because "*a* project in the same area has already been funded" should be strongly resisted. Second, if scientists become engaged in controversial debate, it must not lead to their being discredited. Third, we need to ensure that at least some members of all research teams possess the competencies required to participate in productive public debate.

The interface between researchers, sponsors, and clients needs to be carefully re-assessed. Academia is not a good source of research proposals, since academics generally have little experience of the kind of research needed to inform policy, and little contact with the problems actually experienced by those the policies are intended to benefit.

Administrators, also, having insufficient contact with problems and their potential solution, are often in no position to appreciate the need for relevant work. They often express the need to be certain of outcomes, or a hesitance to commission work unless they know how it is to be carried out. The fundamental problem is that administrators do not wish to be held responsible for risky activities initiated by anyone other than their superiors. Worries concerning "risky" research also lie behind the misguided principle that researchers should provide sponsors with detailed research proposals. Prior knowledge of methods and probable outcomes fosters security on all sides, but it leads to trivial research which fails to advance understanding.

Decisions concerning the research to be undertaken need to be under more direct control of researchers and those aware of problems which need to be researched. Funding should be allocated on the basis of judgments concerning the competence of a given research team to initiate and carry through important innovatory projects. Clearly, such a scenario must allow some means for administrators and the public to alert researchers to issues requiring investigation. Once again, it seems, we reach the conclusion that such research should be organized through "parallel organization" activity.

One informative example comes from a Scottish Council for Research in Education project—*Pupils in Profile*. This was initiated because a number of school principals were concerned that current forms of assessment limited the educational programs they could offer. Despite strong opposition from administrators, the project went ahead and, despite its inability to deliver the tools needed by the principals, documented many difficulties and produced a system of "profile" reporting forms which have since been widely used. Unfortunately, research at the Scottish Council then came to be funded on a contractual basis, and the researchers found themselves unable to follow through to capitalize upon the insights they had developed and or even continue the innovative research style which led to their initial success.

It is not difficult to find examples of the futility of contract research. Two hundred million dollars were spent on evaluations of Headstart and Follow-Through[10.6] designed to satisfy administrators' (changing) criteria, yet these evaluations almost completely failed to advance understanding of the issues. Ironically, the new understanding which *has* been achieved in the area comes almost entirely from the very poorly funded work of Levenstein,[10.7] McClelland[10.8] and Sigel.[10.9]

A mechanism is required to enable the public to influence research activity leading to educational and other policy. It is also too easy for researchers to redefine, in their own terms, problems brought to them by the public. It is therefore necessary to create a mechanism whereby groups of people with a particular—often marginal—perspective, can find researchers who share their viewpoint and ensure that the research continues to be informed by that perspective. Such a mechanism could capitalize on the Information-Technology based networks we have already suggested to supervise public policy.

The Role of Evaluators

Specific problems confront evaluators in their effort to monitor the effectiveness of policies and find ways of improving them. Evaluators frequently find themselves dealing with issues which have little to do with their parent discipline. For example, a good educational evaluator will draw attention to such things as the effects of demarcation disputes between social work and education, the difficulties created by the absence of appropriate transport, the effects of inadequate supplies of materials, and deficits in building design, even though these issues do not relate directly to the specifically *educational* aspects of the policy evaluated.[10.10] Day and Klein[10.11] have argued that one reason for the retention of ineffective policy is that any professional group can always argue that *their* activities *would* be effective if only they were supported by activities in other professional groups. They can also argue that their work ameliorates some problem other than that examined by the evaluators.

A good evaluation gets a rough fix on all important, short and long term outcomes of a particular policy, and some measure of the constraints on its effectiveness: In other words, it involves *systems* analysis. The hallmark of a good evaluation is its *comprehensiveness*, not the accuracy of the particular observations that have been made. Failure to comment on an important consequence of the program, or to draw attention to an important constraint on its effectiveness, constitutes a more serious defect than failure to get an accurate measure of its effect on a single outcome.[10.12]

A good evaluation, then, assesses how effective a program *would* be if it were implemented with and without a context of general understanding of what it is about, with and without proper training, with and without support material, and with and without interference from those fearful of its consequences. It seeks to predict the long-term effects of a program, including negative social and educational effects (such as the development of trained incapacity). Such broadly based work, aimed at achieving an approximate estimation of many variables, cutting across disciplines, and anticipating the future, conflicts with the tenor of academic research. This hints at the serious problems which arise when attempts are made to locate genuine policy research in traditional "academic" institutions.[10.13]

After the results of an evaluation have been disseminated and debated, problems still remain for their translation into effective action. It is unusual for a policy recommendation to be based upon a single research finding. The numerous considerations to be taken into account typically derive from many different domains. Such considerations again underline the importance of network-based management drawing on evaluations conducted by individuals or teams with roots in more than one academic camp.

Career Structures for Those Involved in Research

Researchers often find it necessary to mount political crusades in order to ensure that their work is applied.[10.14] This detracts from the time available to produce the publications deemed necessary for an academic career, and also leads people to doubt the scientific integrity and "impartiality" of the researcher. It is vital that appropriate career structures be developed for those involved in research. These should offer the security researchers need if they are to enter into public debate over controversial issues. They should also offer researchers the flexibility they need to redirect their work when they find they have set out in the wrong direction and the time they need to mull over and make explicit the implications of their observations.

A few words also need to be said about the time scales that are involved in useful policy research. On the one hand, it is necessary to make significant progress in a limited period of time. This cannot be achieved in the individualistic (non-team based) atmosphere characteristic of academe, still less in the one-third time academics usually allocate to research. On the other hand, the time scales involved in doing useful research are much longer than is typically assumed by many sponsoring agencies. Researchers need to pursue problems which were not obvious and to do the conceptual, inventive, work that is needed to find ways of thinking about and tackling them. Many of the problems of the educational system are chronic and have been around for almost a century. They will still be around tomorrow and are not amenable to quick fixes. Enduring issues must be addressed. Crisis type problems tend to have solved themselves (or been shifted elsewhere) by the time "useful" data relating to them become available. Useful research cannot be undertaken in a situation where "priorities" change every couple of years, in which more time has to be devoted to proposal-writing than to carrying out research, in which the interval between the proposal, the report, and the next proposal is insignificant, in which there is little time for exploratory work or developing understanding and new measures prior to rushing into the field, or in which there is several years' delay between researchers identifying a problem and obtaining the funds needed to tackle it.

Scientists need to be encouraged to report (a) work carried out with imperfect tools and imperfect methodology, and (b) their impressions of the policy implications of their work. Without reports containing such data and insights, there will be no discussion of some of the most important policy issues, and without such discussion many important policy implications will be overlooked. Only researchers who have been directly involved in the relevant research are sufficiently familiar with the complexities of a problem to recognize these issues and their implications. Contrary to conventional wisdom, the most important activity to be undertaken by social researchers is, not to feed a few unarguable facts into discussion, but to promote public debate itself.

145

Summary

The reasons for the failure of the educational system to achieve its main goals are numerous, deep-seated, mutually interdependent and interacting, non-obvious, and intractable. Finding ways of overcoming these barriers is critically dependent on the implementation of a great deal of research, and research-based development activity. However, the kind of research required, and the way it is to be carried out, differ markedly from conventional ideas and practice.

The work required features elements commonly associated with both fundamental and applied research. It demands conceptual advances involving new methodology and experimentation, but can only be carried out in the context of theoretically-based, systemic, action. Its execution demands team work over an extended period, but needs to be carried out with a sense of urgency. The work required cannot be carried out in a climate of "publish or perish" or within the short time horizons which currently dominate both universities and applied social research institutes. Nor can it be carried out in the context of the traditional leisured life, "teaching," administration, and individualistic, literature-driven research which once characterized academia.

New institutional arrangements are needed to conduct serious policy-relevant social research. The new understandings that are necessary can only be developed through public debate between protagonists advocating positions based on uncertain foundations. And it will be necessary to establish new relationships between researchers, policy makers, teachers, and the clients and customers of the educational system.

PART III

CHAPTER 11

THE WAY FORWARD

In essence, what we have seen in this book is that the failure of the educational system to achieve its main goals is multiply determined and that that failure contributes to the perpetuation of a society which, at least in the short term, requires its educational system to perform functions which are in sharp tension with the educational activities it manifestly needs to undertake.

The social forces which lead to the narrow educational activities were summarized in graphical form in Diagram 1 at the end of Chapter 7. As was indicated at the time, the Diagram makes it abundantly clear that, if changes are introduced one at a time, their effects will tend to be neutralized, and the changes themselves will tend to be eliminated by other forces operating in the system. This is one reason why curriculum change has in the past tended to be isolated and/or short lived: the only schools which have been able to maintain a distinctive curriculum over an extended period of time have, in one way or another, been able to isolate themselves from forces operating in the rest of the system. Likewise, attempts to change assessment procedures are not only undermined by a lack of understanding of how high-level competencies are to be assessed: They are also rendered invalid by the absence of classroom environments in which the relevant qualities can be fostered and displayed and marginalized by the need to reduce all assessments to a single score which can be used to allocate social position and status.

It follows that if enduring change is to be introduced, it will be necessary to make multi-pronged *systemic* (but not centralized, system-wide) interventions: it will be necessary to introduce *simultaneous* change into the way schools are managed (and especially to take the steps that are needed to create climates of innovation within them), into curriculum, into assessment, into the interface with employers, and into the interface between schools and the community.

Unfortunately, in yet another illustration of Catch-22, immediate attempts to introduce systemic change could not work because there is so little understanding of key issues—of the nature of the qualities that are to be fostered, how they are to be nurtured, and how they are to be assessed, of the nature of the required "parallel organization activity," of the roles of administrators, principals and teachers—because administrators, principals and teachers lack the requisite expectations and competencies, because there is a dearth of appropriate evaluation activity, because the necessary interface between schools and the community has yet to be established, and because, within the current structure, it is so difficult to initiate and conduct research of the kind that is needed.

The points at which one could fruitfully intervene to begin to promote the necessary developments and understandings are indicated by the asterisks in Diagram 1. Additional diagrams could usefully be prepared to show how intervention at these points would produce effects—both positive and negative—elsewhere in the system. Further steps could then be taken to reinforce the positive effects and anticipate and counteract negative reactions.

Most people could contribute in one way or another to intervention at these "leverage points": Everyone can do something to help to promote a wider debate in the media. Everyone can strive to influence local school systems. Most people could form, or contribute to, groups to put pressure on congressmen. They could press to have recruitment into teaching based on the ability to facilitate growth rather than on qualifications which primarily index the willingness to regurgitate what "authorities" want to hear. They could try to persuade employers to change their selection criteria. They could campaign to get test agencies to invest in the R&D required to broaden the range of their products. They could take legal action against test agencies for damaging people's lives and careers and society at large. They could press for social change so that there is less need for schools

149

to manufacture discriminations which compel participation in the useless activities of which modern society is so largely composed.

The most important single change they could try to bring into being would, however, involve getting federal and state governments to change the philosophy which informs their current thinking about how the system is to be managed. The need, both within the educational system and outside it, is to create a climate which facilitates development, rather than one in which it is assumed that those in authority should prescribe the activities to be carried out by public servants and teachers and then check up to find out whether those instructions have been obeyed. The new arrangements would include a network-based structure to supervise the public service, tools to run the educational system, and the public service in general, more effectively and a support structure to conduct the necessary research.

Technological change is also extremely important. Teachers teach, and pupils work toward the goals that are *assessed*. Teachers and administrators do those things for which they will be credited in staff appraisal systems, and teachers attend only to those classroom processes they can monitor. Teachers need tools to help them administer individualized, competency-oriented, developmental programs. Such tools would help them to identify and harness pupils' motives, create individualized programs, monitor the results, and record the outcomes. The availability of easy-to-use tools in these areas would transform education, regardless of whether steps were taken to overcome the other barriers to effective education which have been identified in this book.

However, the most difficult, but vitally important, task facing national, state, and local governments is to initiate the developments needed to create a society in which there would be no need for schools to perform their latent sociological functions. These functions include (a) the legitimization of the rationing of privilege, (b) the advancement of those most prepared to do whatever is necessary to secure that advancement, and (c) the manufacturing of useless work and the creation of discriminations which compel participation in both the "educational" system itself and the institutions of modern society. Ironically, the development and dissemination of the understandings needed to divert the educational system away from these functions, and toward the real goals of education, is unmistakably a task for the educational system itself. Unfortunately, as we saw in Chapter 5, Robinson[11.1] has shown that even a relatively innocuous attempt to address this agenda threatened vested interests to such an extent that a concerted campaign was established to crush the activity. There is no reason to suppose that future activity in the area would not meet with a similar response. There are, however, a number of new features in the situation which might lead to a different outcome: (1) We can now anticipate, and prepare for, the reaction of those who have a major interest in the perpetuation of the system; (2) there is now much more widespread dissatisfaction with the educational system; (3) there is now a much wider awareness that the way our society is organized will have to change dramatically; and (4) it is now clear that major social reform is essential to even the relatively short-term interest of those who are most likely to resist change.[11.2]

It will now be apparent that one of the reasons why the reform of education has proved to be so difficult is that it involves the reform of government and society.

It follows from the observations made in this book that, if we are to translate our social and educational values into effect, we will need, above all, to analyze the workings of our society with a view to identifying leverage points at which it would be possible for us to intervene for the common good. To do this, each of us could do worse than begin by asking ourselves, as individuals: "What are my social and educational values?" "What prevents **me** from translating those values into effect?" "What single thing can **I** say, do, or change that is likely to influence the current situation? "[11.3]

151

NOTES

2.1. Morton-Williams, Finch *et al* (1968); Morton-Williams, Raven and Ritchie (1971); Ritchie and Morton-Williams (1971); Sharp (1972); Raven *et al* (1975, 1975); Raven (1977); Raven (1980); Raven, Johnstone and Varley (1985)

2.2. Bill *et al* (1974); Johnston and Bachman (1976); CES (1977); De-Landsheere (1977); MacBeath *et al* (1981); Flanagan and Russ-Eft (1975); Gray *et al* (1983)

2.3. Goodlad (1983)

2.4. Flanagan (1978)

2.5. Johnston and Bachman (1976)

2.6. The objectives were in fact divided into two halves so that no respondent would be confronted by too long a list. For details of sample sizes etc, see Raven, Hannon *et al* (1975) and for a more detailed discussion see Raven (1977).

2.7. Flanagan (1978)

2.8. Bachman *et al* (1978)

2.9. Csikszentmihalyi and LeFevre (1989)

2.10. Flanagan (1976)

2.11. It is important to distinguish this use of the word "values" from the main usage in this book. By and large we will be concerned with *behavior* which the individual finds engaging and motivating and can therefore be said to value. Some behaviors - such as those which conserve resources and preserve the environment may be valued because of their long-term consequences. We will be concerned with ways in which people can be encouraged to develop their own moral codes rather than with ways of inculcating them. Nevertheless we will be unable to entirely avoid the question of *teaching* values because some people *want* to to be taught strict rules to apply to the conduct of their lives.

2.12. Morton-Williams *et al* (1968). A more broadly based comparative table, with data from the many populations which had been surveyed by that time appears in Raven (1977). Goodlad's (1984) results confirm the general conclusion, but the results are much less clear cut owing to the methodology adopted.

2.13. Wells Foshay has pointed out that the list does not contain many aims dealing with qualities that are required for full self-realization. For example, few deal with introverted awareness - awareness of the self and being part of a vastly larger sphere of being. Not only do few of the items deal with ensuring that pupils have experience of self-transcendence, few even deal with ensuring that pupils have experience of expressive activities which might engage them and, as one student put it, 'be good for my soul'. One wonders what support there would be for such objectives as: "Ensure that you have experience of the wonder and awe which can come from contemplating nature, music or art"; "Ensure that you have experience of the new lease of life which can arise from musical experience"; "Ensure that you have experience of being part of a process greater than yourself"; "Ensure that you have experience of a range of the emotions which can be evoked by literature"; "Ensure that you have experience of the feelings which are associated with accomplishing something very worthwhile" (Maslow's peak experiences); "Help you to develop the capacity to clarify and express your feelings"; "Help you to learn how to behave in ways which are in accord with, and express, your feelings"; "Put you in touch with your inner needs and feelings and teach you how to express them"; "Enable you to experience feelings and emotions that you have not had before"; "Enable you to experience inner peace and harmony"; "Enable you to experience emotions like hatred, fear, love, and awe"; and "Help you to find ways of expressing your being in science, art, music, words, movement, friendship, and song." One problem with such formulations of objectives having to do with self-awareness and self-transcendence is that they tend to be viewed as relating chiefly to artistic and mystical activities. Students studying the sciences tend to learn to abhor what they regard as "wishy-washy," "artsy-craftsy," pretentious, artistic material whereas, as Foshay (1991) has shown, competence in dealing with these processes is crucial to the student's ultimate success in scientific or mathematical endeavors. Furthermore, support for such objectives would only exacerbate a problem that will be highlighted later in this book - namely that important feelings and experiences only come into play while people are undertaking activities which are important to them - yet such activities are conspicuous by their absence in most schools and introducing them poses a host of serious dilemmas.

2.14. Bruner (1965); Curriculum Development Associates (1969/70); Nuffield Science (1967); Schools Council Integrated Science Project (1970-72); Schools Council Humanities Project (1970-72).

2.15. eg, Newton Public Schools (1972); Wright (1950). See Fraley (1981) for a review of these projects.

3.1. This material is presented in detail in *Competence in Modern Society* (Raven, 1984).

3.2. Klemp *et al* (1977); Klemp and McClelland (1986); see also Jaques (1976); McClelland and Burnham (1976); Winter (1979).

3.3. Raven and Dolphin (1978)

3.4. Graham, Raven and Smith (1987)

3.5. Raven and Dolphin (1978)

3.6. Sykes (1969)

3.7. Van Beinum (1965)

3.8. Fivars and Gosnell (1966)

3.9. See McClelland (1961); Burgess and Pratt (1970); Schwartz (1987).

3.10. McClelland and Dailey (1973, 1974)

3.11. MacKinnon (1962); Schon (1987)

3.12. Dunn and Hamilton (1985)

3.13. Schon (1987)

3.14. McClelland and Dailey (1973, 1974); Raven (1984). Also, what is most interesting about Schwartz's (1987) study is that, although he was nominally studying businessmen's responsiveness to changes in their environment, their ultimate success in reaching the objectives the country (ie, civil servants) had set for them was dependent on the quality of the civil servants' judgments both in establishing the objectives and on their correct understanding of how to manipulate prices and grants in order to get "independent entrepreneurs" to achieve these objectives. Their job is, it seems, to manage both businessmen and the economy.

3.15. Price *et al* (1971)

3.16. Taylor and Barron (1963); McClelland (1962)

3.17. Beuret and Webb (1983); Fores and Pratt (1980)

3.18. Raven (1984)

3.19. Flanagan and Burns (1955)

3.20. ITRU (1979)

3.21. Morton-Williams *et al* (1968)

3.22. Grannis (1983)

3.23. Bachman *et al* (1971, 1978). Employment in *large* factories and offices are the only general exceptions to the statement that work is, in general, better and more developmental than being at school. But far fewer people are employed in these organizations than is commonly assumed and such organizations are, in any case, rapidly being automated.

.24. Huff *et al* (1982); Klemp *et al* (1980); Schneider *et al* (1981); Raven *et al* (1985)

.25. Raven (1973); Raven and Litton (1976); Litton and Raven (1977/82); Raven and Whelan (1976). It is pertinent to the argument of this book to note the role of feelings and hunches in "intellectual" activity: we collected these data - and indeed much of the data on pupils' values and teachers' perceptions of them that are reported elsewhere in this book - because we somehow *felt* that they were important. It was only many years later that we were able to articulate *why* the data were important - why they should have been collected and what they really told us about the way to conceptualize the determinants of behavior and the functioning of the educational system. This is not only contrary to widely held beliefs about how research should proceed but also to the current emphasis on cognitive activity as a basis for action.

26. See Raven and Whelan (1976); Raven and Litton (1976); Litton and Raven (1977/82).

27. Flanagan and Russ-Eft (1975). Our own replication of it is published in Raven (1980).

28. I have discussed this set of issues much more fully in Raven (1984, 1987).

29. Price *et al* (1971); Taylor *et al* (1963)

30. Payne *et al* (1979)

3.31. Hope (1984)

3.32. This is not to imply that it is not important for there to be some shared concerns and values. Our data and that collected by McClelland's team (1961) shows that a shared concern with finding better ways of doing things and important new things to do has a dramatic effect on economic and social development, and, conversely, that divisiveness and an arrogant attachment to one's own point of view result in endemic conflict. All of these issues need to be surfaced and resolved if we are to develop an effective educational policy. The point here is to underline that we need a *variety* of goals in education and that we need to collect good data before we set about imposing our values on others.

4.1. Taylor (1974, 1976, 1986, 1988), Schlichter (1986), and Hatch and Gardner (1990) have shown that, once one sets out to look for a wider range of talents in children, it is possible to identify real, idiosyncratic, gifts in virtually all children. Further, even if one resorts to variable-based assessments of only the 7 or 8 talents that each was concerned with, the correlation between most of these abilities is less than .2: ie, 96% of the variance is *not* common variance: people who are good at one thing are *not* good at doing other things.

4.2. Raven (1984, 1991); but see also Raven (1988, 1988, 1992). Gardner (1983, 1985, 1987) has made a number of similar points about assessment but does not recognize just how many talents there are, just how important it is to create situations which tap people's values in order to lead them to develop and display their talents, or how inadequate is observed behavior as an index of the talents which people possess - and therefore the need to, in some sense, get inside their heads.

5.1. Goodlad (1983); Flanagan (1978); Johnston (1973); ORACLE; HMI (Scotland) (1980); HMI (1990); Raven et al (1985)

5.2. Goodlad (1983). Earlier American studies coming to the same conclusion include those of Flanagan (1978), Johnston (1973) and Johnston and Bachman (1976). A more detailed critique of Goodlad's conclusions than that which follows will be found in Raven (1986).

5.3. Flanagan (1978)

5.4. Johnston (1973)

5.5. See also Flanagan (1978) and Bachman et al (1971).

5.6. HMI (Scotland) (1980); HMI (1990); MacBeath et al (1981); ORACLE

5.7. Torney et al (1975); Raven and Litton (1976); Raven (1988)

5.8. Throughout my career as a researcher, the worlds of academe and administration have been pervaded by statements to the effect that "Yes, it used to be like that, but, in the last couple of years all has changed." These beliefs have generally turned out to be unfounded. Two examples may be cited. One concerns primary education. The group which is responsible for quality control in British schools - Her Majesty's Inspectors of Schools - believed that their efforts had led to substantial change in primary education. And the schools they took visitors to confirmed them in this opinion. Yet when, in 1979, they undertook their own survey in a representative sample of schools they

156

discovered that there had been virtually no change in 40 years (HMI, 1980). Par for the course, they now believe that the steps they have taken since have led to the desired changes! In the US Goodlad (1974, 1983) and Fraley (1981) found that, despite the advocacy of Progressive Education over very many years, little had changed. The second example comes from teacher training. Since 1945, there have been a series of major enquiries into teacher training in Scotland. All identified virtually the same problems and made recommendations to deal with them. After each, most people (other than the students) believed that these recommendations had been implemented and that the problems had been solved. However, yet another committee (Sneddon, 1978) identified exactly the same problems - and made yet another set of recommendations to deal with them. Unfortunately, these were either unrelated to the nature of the problems or ignored constraints which would nullify their effect (Raven, 1987). Other examples could be cited. Time after time, as the truth has dawned, yet another tranch of reforms - based on a new "commonsense" understanding of the problems and their solutions has been introduced in a blaze of hype. Needless to say, lacking a substantive basis in policy analysis and research, it, too, has failed. The whole process forces one to take seriously both Chomsky's claim that the role of intellectuals and academics is the same as that of court jesters in the middle ages, and Popkewitz's (1982) claim that the function of curriculum development is to divert attention from fundamental and intractable problems which teachers would otherwise be unable to tolerate.

5.9.   These include the reports of DES (1989). In the first place, the concerns which are expressed in these reports are, on the whole, so unchanged that it is difficult to believe that new goals are being pursued. Next, those which do embrace different concerns are none too positive: "Secondary school work is not as good as it might be. There is an over-emphasis on content, while opportunities for pupils to make decisions, think creatively, and engage in discussion are unduly limited. This is similar to the position in the country as a whole." When they turn to activities which might have been used to foster the kinds of qualities we have been concerned with in this book they become even more outspoken. Mini-enterprise activities are, for example, described as badly organized and strongly criticized for their muddled thinking even about such fundamental issues as profitability (but note the emphasis on content!). Still more generally, the *New Curriculum* in England - which is not noted for its emphasis on the wider goals of education - is said by HMI to have been badly implemented in about one third of schools ... and the work of the other schools is described in such a rosy way that it is impossible to believe that the kinds of activities that are described occur in most schools.

5.10.   Morton-Williams *et al* (1968); Raven (1977)

5.11.   De Landsheere (1977)

5.12.   Raven (1977); Bill *et al* (1974)

5.13.   HMI (Scotland) (1980); MacBeath *et al* (1981); Gray *et al* (1983); CES (1977); Gow and MacPherson (1980)
5.14.   Bill *et al* (1974)
5.15.   Grannis (1983)
5.16.   Bachman *et al* (1978)
5.17.   Flanagan (1978)
5.18.   Robinson *et al* (1969, 1969)
5.19.   Bachman *et al* (1978)
5.20.   Tyler, L. *in* Flanagan (1978)
5.21.   Raven (1977)
5.22.   Raven (1977, 1980)
5.23.   Flanagan (1978)
5.24.   Collins (1979)
5.25.   CES (1977)
5.26.   Raven (1976, 1977)
5.27.   Goodlad (1983)
5.28.   Raven, Hannon *et al* (1975); Raven (1977)
5.29.   Torney *et al* (1975); Raven and Litton (1976)
5.30.   Raven *et al* (1985); Raven and Varley (1984)
5.31.   Berg (1973)
5.32.   Jencks *et al* (1973)
5.33.   Flanagan (1978)
5.34.   Bachman *et al* (1978)
5.35.   Collins (1979)
5.36.   Flanagan (1978)
5.37.   Schon (1987)
5.38.   Reimer (1971)
5.39.   Holt (1977)
5.40.   Goodman (1962)
5.41.   Freire (1970)
5.42.   Winter and McClelland (1963)
5.43.   Freedman and Berg (1978)
5.44.   Bill *et al* (1974)
5.45.   Collins (1979)
5.46.   Raven (1977, 1980)
5.47.   Willis (1977)
5.48.   Tomlinson and Tenhouten (1976). There may be a cultural difference here. I have the distinct impression that American children are more likely to learn how to use the system for their own advantage, while many more British children learn that the educational system is a fraud - that it is not what it seems to be - and generalize that observation so that it becomes "nothing in society is what it purports to be - and is usually the opposite" and apply that observation to the workings of government, insurance, defense, health care, etc.

5.49. Hope (1984)

5.50. Just as there is more food value in the packages of breakfast cereals than in their contents and what is being sold is the hype and the packaging, so most of what is sold - from cars to insurance packages - consists largely of images and fails to deliver the benefits that are claimed. Education, mental health care, and defense are conspicuously fraudulent activities in the public domain.

5.51. Bernstein (1971, 1975)

5.52. Hope (1984)

5.53. Berg (1973)

5.54. Goodman (1962)

5.55. Tomlinson and Tenhouten (1976)

5.56. Nuttgens (1988)

5.57. Bernstein (1971)

5.58. Dore (1976)

5.59. Hope (1984)

5.60. Kohn (1969)

5.61. Kinsey (1948)

5.62. Bouchard and McGue (1990); McGue and Bouchard (1989); Waller, Kojetin *et al* (1989)

5.63. Tellegen *et al* (1988); Stassen *et al* (1988)

5.64. Berg (1973)

5.65. Kanter (1985)

5.66. Raven and Litton (1976)

5.67. Schon (1987)

5.68. Nuttgens (1988)

5.69. The correct word is "hegemony" but experience shows that it alienates many readers. It is not just the concept itself that is the problem, but also the way in which it is embedded in the organization and framing of educational knowledge and structures: that is to say in the divisional structure of university "Departments" and the criteria which are applied in connection with promotion within that structure.

5.70. Hogan (1990)

5.71. Nuttgens (1988)

5.72. Hope (1984)

5.73. Chomsky (1987)

5.74. McClelland *et al* (1958)

5.75. Popkewitz (1982)

6.1. See Raven (1977, 1984) for summaries.

6.2. Raven (1980)

6.3. Raven *et al* (1985); Raven (1987)

6.4. Raven (1984); Raven and Dolphin (1978)

6.5. McClelland (1961, 1964, 1965, 1982, 1982); McClelland *et al* (1969); Winter and McClelland (1963, 1981)

6.6.   Kohn (1969, 1977); see also Burns *et al* (1984).

6.7.   Klemp *et al* (1977)

6.8.   Huff *et al* (1982)

6.9.   Gallimore (1985)

6.10.   Flanagan (1978) found that most 30-year-olds could identify at least one teacher who had led them to clarify their values and released latent competencies.

6.11.   Collins (1979) found that high-level competencies had been developed on the job.

6.12.   See, for example, Gardner (1983, 1987, 1990).

6.13.   Bachman *et al* (1971, 1978)

6.14.   Jackson (1986)

6.15.   Winter *et al* (1981)

6.16.   Note the way in which this supports Schon's (1987) observations on the hegemony of the technico-rational model of competence.

6.17.   See eg, Aikin (1942).

6.18.   Bernstein (1975). There is, of course, a deeper version of Bernstein's argument. This is that the objective was to create a mechanism which would select and advance those who were both able to work out what one needed to do to obtain the preferment of one's superiors and who were willing to do whatever was necessary. This ability, crucially important to both advancement in, and the operation of, modern society, includes the ability to justify one's behavior by mouthing the right words (in this case about useful education) while actually engaging in the activity for other reasons. We may note in passing that in learning to do these things pupils would be learning to labor in a much more important way than the pupils described by Willis (1977).

6.19.   Cremin (1961), Fraley (1981), and Ravitch (1974) have provided useful summaries of the Progressive Education movement. Dewey (1899, 1910, 1916) seems to have been preoccupied with fostering the skills of the research scientist (the ability to conceptualize, analyse and experiment) on the one hand and with creating democratic classrooms on the other. His writing does not encourage teachers to make use of multiple-talent concepts of ability (for example by encouraging them to think about a wide range of alternative talents which schools might foster), still less encourage them to foster different competencies in different children. Most of Kilpatrick's writing (eg, *Foundations of Method*, 1926) is obscure in the extreme, but in his 1918 text on *The Project Method* he indicates that, in translating a plan into a reality, pupils should practice proposing, planning, executing and judging. These are high-level competencies, but Kilpatrick does not analyse them or present them in a way which would encourage teachers to reflect on what it means to, eg, plan and execute, or on the counseling which is necessary if pupils are to practice (and thereby develop) these competencies in the course of undertaking activities they care about. Counts (1932) and Rugg (in a range of texts for pupils) seem to have set out to introduce *particular* understandings of socio-politico-economic processes. The majority of "Progressive Educators" have been even less specific about the knowledge they have been trying to inculcate or the qualities which should be fostered in pupils. Indeed most have been explicitly opposed to any attempt to specify objectives. However this majority is made up of two very different groups of people. One group may be termed the "romanticists." They believe that children should be left on their own to thereby learn "instinctively" what is important to them. A larger group is clearer about what it is opposed to than what it is for. These teachers have been so appalled by either or both (i) the effects on most children, and thence on society, of the competitive and self-advancement-centered climate which permeates most classrooms and (ii) the selection of a small number of pupils who possess a very limited range of not particularly valuable "academic" competencies (which do not in fact deserve to be so described) for advancement into the most prestigeous and influential positions in society, that they have been more concerned with destroying the competitive climate and the limited "standards" than with putting something else in their place. (It is this group which is responsible for the cult of mediocrity which is widely associated with Progressive Education.) What is important from the point of view of this footnote is, however, that, for one or other of these reasons, the majority of Progressive Educators believe that any attempt to state objectives would reintroduce competitiveness. Most attempts to *implement* "Progressive Education" seem to have been an appalling mess: Barth (1972), Aikin (1942), Rathbone (1971), Rugg (1926), Rugg and Schumaker (1928), Wright (1950, 1958). The "bible" of the Progressive Education Movement (the 1926 Handbook of the NSSE) nowhere identifies the competencies which are to be fostered, how they are to be fostered, or how they are to be assessed for either formative or summative purposes. French *et al* (1957), Stratemeyer *et al* (1947), Caswell and Campbell (1935), Tyler (1936), and the Educational Policies Commission (1938) do attempt to identify goals, but have muddled together goals at a wide variety of levels, the frameworks are not multiple-talent frameworks, and the goals are only weakly linked to curriculum processes. Most accounts of classroom processes focus on encouraging students to take "democratic" decisions within the compulsory attendance framework of schools (a framework which deprives pupils of citizenship rights and most of the sources of power and influence [eg, the option to withdraw and the opportunity to influence decisions and gain treatment suited to their own priorities through the marketplace] which are open to people in capitalist "democracies") and in which teachers could not allow students to implement many decisions which would command majority support from pupils, on "discovering" low-level everyday facts about the local area which have nothing to do with each other, little bearing on any area of organized endeavor, which the pupils are unlikely to need in the future, which the teacher already knows, and which are mostly "discovered" from books, sometimes from highly directed field trips, and sometimes from "discussions" which involve guessing what the teacher has in mind. The recurrent eulogizing references to democracy in this context are not only somewhat nauseating in themselves, they conjure up images of the many crimes against mankind which have been committed in the name of protecting and advancing "democracy" and in this way may have alienated many potential adherents to competency-oriented education. Among the few partial exceptions to the rather damning picture are the writings of Barnes and her colleagues at the Lincoln school (Barnes and Young, 1932; Tippett *et al* 1927), although, even here, Bestor (1953), an ex-pupil of the school, has taken the school to task for offering courses which focussed on teaching non-generalizable everyday knowledge instead of encouraging pupils to make contact with academic disciplines (or, we might add, developing high-level competencies). Modern students of education are, however, unlikely even to come into contact with the more widely-oriented writing in the area since it is not referenced in, still less embedded in, more recent writings on Progressive Education (eg, Barth [1972], Ravitch [1974, 1983], or the 1985 *International Encyclopaedia of Education* (Husen and Postlethwaite, 1985).

6.20. None of the teachers Bennett (1976) asked to define "Progressive Education" did so in terms of distinctive goals and, as is well known, Bennett subsequently concluded from his classroom observations that most "open" classrooms were a mess. The failure to articulate non-knowledge-of-content goals is well illustrated in Curtis's *Boats* Project (Tippett *et al* 1927; Cremin, 1961). This would appear to have remained heavily content- and skill- oriented, with a hint of *introducing* pupils to new interests. It contains little suggestion of using interests to *foster* competencies. Dewey seems to have been content to evaluate projects designed to encourage experimentation in terms of their contribution to knowledge rather than in terms of the competencies developed in the process. Likewise, he seems to have been content if "democratic" processes were enacted in classrooms. He does not seem to have set down the competencies and understandings required for democratic functioning.

6.21. Raven *et al* (1985)

6.22. The Eight Year Study (Aikin, 1942) made a pioneering attempt to tackle some of the assessment issues. However its work was not followed through and the crucial importance of assessment from the point of view of: (a) enabling teachers to achieve their goals, (b) enabling students to identify the benefits, and (c) harnessing the sociological forces which determine what happens in schools through the certification process was not recognized.

6.23. *International Encyclopaedia of Education* (Husen and Postlethwaite, 1985)

6.24. Travers (1973); Wittrock (1986)

6.25. Taylor (1971, 1976)

6.26. (a) Although this example comes from elementary schools, a great deal of material on how high school teachers can foster high-level competencies by changing the way they teach their subjects, through interdisciplinary and project-based studies, and through special courses is

162

available in Raven (1977). (b) Mathematics was not fully integrated into this scheme. However, the problems which this teacher had in trying to integrate mathematics into her interdisciplinary teaching actually highlight neither deficiencies in the philosophy of interdisciplinary education, nor deficiencies in this teacher's competence, but the need to radically re-think mathematics education.

6.27.   Barnes and Young (1932)

6.28.   Gardner (1990) and Walters and Gardner (1986) likewise assert that "finding some topic or skill with which one feels 'connected' is the single most important event in a student's life." Flanagan (1978) makes a similar observation from his data from the *Project Talent* follow-up about the lifetime effects of schooling.

6.28.   Curtis, see Cremin (1961)

6.29.   See also Jackson (1986)

6.30.   Bandura (1977)

6.31.   Gardner (1990) has suggested that working with only one person who shares their concerns and models appropriate behavior may enable the pupil to sustain the behavior even when he or she is confronted with the mindless activities which occupy so much time at school and in the wider society. This is an important suggestion which is supported by Flanagan's (1978) observation that most adults are able to cite at least one person who changed their lives in this way in their youth. Unfortunately, Gardner does not seem to recognize the full range of competencies the development of which can be facilitated in this way or the importance of the shared valuation of particular behavior.

6.32.   Jackson (1986)

6.33.   Raven (1977). This book documents ways in which high school teachers can foster high-level competencies by teaching their subjects in particular ways, through project work, through interdisciplinary studies, and by running theoretically based programs.

6.34.   Winter *et al* (1981)

6.35.   On reading this statement in an earlier draft of the book Stanley Nisbet wrote to say that a survey he once conducted in Glasgow University came to the same conclusion.

6.36.   Gardner (1990) and Duckworth (1987) have also stressed the importance of children developing their own mathematical notations.

6.37.   Parker (1894); Dewey (1902); Kilpatrick (1918); Bourne (1916); Rugg and Schumaker (1928); Mississippi State Department (1936); Aikin (1942); Cremin (1961); Newton Public Schools (1972); Barth (1972); Fraley (1981). Once again, Stanley Nisbet has drawn my attention to a process which may have contributed to this oversight. The claim to be child-centered in itself says nothing about whether a teacher focuses on conveying content or nurturing high-level competencies in his or her interaction with the individual child. Since much discussion of the issues surrounding Progressive Education have been couched in these terms, this may have enabled more teachers to have engaged in competency-oriented education than is immediately obvious. This process of concealment may have been exacerbated by another. Even a teacher who focuses on competence, will, *in his or her interactions with the pupils*, focus mainly on content - on butterflies and their habitats, on what people were talking about and so on. It is only when they engage in a "higher level" discussion - such as about the students' motives and talents and how they can be harnessed to contribute to a group project or when they discuss the educational process itself - that they will publicly focus on the competencies to be nurtured. Unfortunately, neither our own observations nor the data available support these hypotheses.

7.1. See Raven (1977, 1984, 1988); Raven *et al* (1985) for our contributions to resolving these difficulties.

7.2. Dewey (1902)

7.3. Aikin (1942)

7.4. Caswell (1942)

7.5. Whiting (1972)

7.6. Fraley (1981)

7.7. Bruner (1965); Curriculum Development Associates (1969/70); Nuffield Science (1967); Schools Council Integrated Science Project (1970-72); Schools Council Humanities Project (1970-72)

7.8. See Hargreaves (1988) for a discussion of these movements.

7.9. MSC (1984)

7.10. The Educational Reform Bill (Her Majesty's Government, 1988)

7.11. I have discussed the inadequacy of the latter measures, as introduced by the Government, as a mechanism for school improvement in Raven (1989). The goals are wildly unrealistic and the proposed assessment procedures have drained off enormous resources and goodwill - but cannot work without a substantive research base. Yet the one thing which is not proposed is *any* kind of fundamental research.

7.12. IEA: Comber and Keeves (1973); Purves (1973); Thorndike (1973)

7.13. Raven *et al* (1985)

7.14. The development and provision of such tools is not as unrealistic as may at first sight appear because the computers which are required to run programs designed to elicit the relevant information from pupils and suggest appropriate individualized experiences to both pupils and teachers are now widely available. Nevertheless the development of the necessary tools does remain dependent on the wider adoption and refinement of the framework for thinking about the nature and development of competence which has emerged in the course of our work and is summarized in Raven (1984). Work is currently in hand to develop a kit of assessment procedures which are designed to introduce teachers to this framework, to nurture in them an understanding of the classroom processes which are required to foster high level competencies, and key features of "parallel organization activity."

7.15. Raven (1977)

7.16. Raven (1977, 1980). Under the circumstances, the wonder is that any school pupils are willing to enroll in genuinely developmental activities. But, they are. However, as Schon noted, and as is widely reported, it becomes increasingly difficult to persuade students further up in the educational system to devote time to such activities. They know too well that advancement, whether in the educational system or outside, is not achieved by demonstrating occupational (let alone personal or civic) competence but by discerning and saying the right things to the right people. (Sternberg [1986] has included a knowledge of what to do to secure promotion in the academic world as one of his varieties of "intelligence." [Thus, incidentally, confounding values, problem-solving ability, and acquired information].)

7.17. Raven (1977); Dore (1976); Broadfoot (1979)

7.18. Raven (1977)

7.19. Morton-Williams *et al* (1966)

7.20. Dore (1976)

7.21. Raven (1980); Raven *et al* (1985)

7.22. Morton-Williams *et al* (1966)

7.23. Note that this comment applies with equal force to the competence areas which are currently embedded within the curriculum - ie, to the 3Rs. It is easy to see that - as is spelled out in Raven (1989) - the teaching of reading in particular and the development of the ability to communicate is seriously hampered by teachers' failure to relate what they are doing to children's interests and preoccupations. There is no doubt about the need for modularized knowledge to support competency oriented programs.

7.24. Raven (1980); Raven *et al* (1985)

7.25. Bachman *et al* (1978); Jackson (1986)

7.26. Raven (1984)

7.27. Raven (1977)

7.28. Raven (1977); Sigel (1985); Pellegrini *et al* (1985); Burns *et al* (1984); Miller *et al* (1985, 1986)

7.29. Hope (1984); Payne *et al* (1979)

7.30. See Raven (1984) for the evidence that high-level competencies are value-laden and involve social and political beliefs. See Raven (1980) for a discussion of the importance of coming to terms with values.

7.31. See Raven (1989) for a fuller discussion of this issue.

7.32. See Raven (1980, 1987, 1989).

7.33. Hogan (1990) has noted that the available evidence suggests that about half of those managers who appear to be competent, confident, intelligent, poised, and skilled in human relations, either: (a) destroy the careers of competent subordinates in order to minimise challenge and competition, (b) destroy the developmental potential of their sections (ie, get rid of the time and the personnel required for the "parallel organization activity" which is required for innovation and to provide for the future) in order to seem able to reduce costs and appear "efficient," or (c) refuse to take important decisions which affect the future of the organization because these would result in their becoming unpopular and thus jeopardize their future.

7.34.   I have the impression that more people in the UK than the US have observed that the educational system is not what it seems to be and generalized this observation to other aspects of society and chosen to resist, whereas in the US more students have simply accepted the mythology, and, as a result, failed to question market mythology, religious mythology, and democratic mythology.

7.35.   Actually, more people involved in the useless tasks of education, insurance, defense industries, trade, *is* economic development. Thus growth of education does not lead to GNP; educational employment is *part of* GNP.

7.36.   Robinson (1983)

7.37.   Bellini (1980)

7.38.   Chomsky (1987)

7.39.   Kanter (1985)

7.40.   Toffler (1980)

7.41.   Schon (1971/73)

7.42.   Ferguson (1980)

7.43.   The downtrodden and rather ineffectual images which teachers have of themselves are documented in Raven (1977) and the fact that these are communicated to pupils is documented in Raven and Varley (1984).

7.44.   Morgan (1986)

8.1.   Hogan (1990) has documented how three types of self-interested people destroy their organizations for the sake of personal advancement.

8.2.   It may be noted that a Japanese delegation visited Britain and America in the 1870s and were so horrified at the inefficiency of market management that they set up a system of explicit management which has been in place - and highly successful - ever since.

8.3.   Something which has been noticeable in Britain, but which may not have been so characteristic of the United States, is that when large firms get into financial difficulties they are bought by the state at rock-bottom prices. It is the state which then sets about modernizing them, pouring in millions of pounds, and then, when they are viable, selling them back into private ownership.

8.4.   Dockrell (1991)

8.5.   See Dockrell (1991).

8.6.   It is important to note that Kanter's research was not confined to private sector organizations.

8.7.   Gardner's (1987) use of the term "cultures of intelligence" to refer to cultures which utilize people with different preoccupations and areas of competence in a complementary way to generate new ideas and ways of doing things is technically correct. This can be shown by considering the concept of "Military Intelligence." Military Intelligence is a noun which is used to designate a body of tentative knowledge. The qualities required to develop this knowledge include the ability to seek out, collate, reinterpret, and piece together, scraps of unreliable information in order to perceive something new. They include the ability to make good judgments about which scraps of information to rely on and which to discard. These judgments have to be made in the light of impressions of the reliability of the sources of the information and the emerging whole. But the qualities required to establish military intelligence also include the motivation and the ability to do such things as set up and manage networks of contacts to obtain the information, the ability to supply those contacts with appropriate guidance as to the kind of information that should be sought and is likely to be useful, and the ability to pry information out of people who do not want to part with it. This process clearly involves the exercise of the two components of g identified by Spearman (1923) ie, eductive and reproductive ability. But it also involves the effective use of accumulated specialist knowledge of military operations, people, and systems. It involves the ability to discriminate the significant from the insignificant, the ability to engage in the political activity required to set up and manage an effective system for trawling for information, and the ability to select and develop staff to perform those roles. Cultures of intelligence therefore involve the complementary (if not spontaneously cooperative) exercise of competencies which go well beyond even the seven intelligences discussed by Gardner, never mind the much more limited kind of intelligence that comes to mind when the term is used. It is therefore preferable to describe the sometimes stressful cultures in which a range of distinctive but complementary competencies are utilized to produce new things to do, new ways of doing things, and new ways of thinking about things as cultures of enterprise or innovation rather than as cultures of intelligence.

There is, however, a sense in which none of these terms conjure up quite the right image. None of them call to mind the ideas evoked by the term "developmental environment." Yet teachers need to be able to develop the confidence and the competencies required to undertake the diverse tasks required for innovation. In using the term "cultures of enterprise and innovation" we wish, therefore, to conflate the two meanings of "culture."

8.8.   Rogers (1962/1983)

8.9.   Litwin et al (1967); Klemp et al (1977)

8.10.   Adams and Burgess (1989)

8.11.   Rogers (1962) has provided a useful account of these processes at work.

8.12.   Schon (1972/73)

8.13.   Jaques (1989)

8.14.   Jaques (1989) has argued that it is the task of the manager *once removed* to undertake such guidance, placement, and counseling, because only he (or she) has the breadth of vision and understanding that is necessary.

8.15. See also Jaques (1989).

8.16. *Records of Achievement* (Adams and Burgess, 1989) contribute to this process because they lead people to make explicit their own understanding of the process of which they form a part - and of their contribution to that process - and then to discuss those perceptions with their colleagues and superiors.

8.17. For a fuller discussion see Raven (1984).

8.18. Raven *et al* (1985); Raven (1987); Huff *et al* (1982); Schneider *et al* (1981)

8.19. The word political is used to signal (a) that these coalitions are designed to influence wider social processes and (b) that the groups are not made up of people who share all their concerns and interests, but groups of people who have in common the aim of changing certain processes in the wider society.

8.20. Raven *et al* (1985); Raven (1987); Huff *et al* (1982); Klemp *et al* (1977); Schneider *et al* (1981)

8.21. That these fears are well founded is illustrated in Raven (1988, 1991). Adams *et al* (1981) clearly demonstrate this effect in the polytechnic they studied, while much of my own research has in a sense documented the effects which 'payment by results' has in education when very few of the most important outcomes show up on the measures; a much fuller discussion of the damaging effects of the limited range of formal evaluation procedures will be found in Raven (1984, 1985, 1991).

8.22. Harlen's (1984) research shows that this is indeed the case.

8.23. The assertion that there was no evidence that the pupils were doing these things is dependent on introducing and applying criteria that the teachers were **not** using (Johnstone and Raven, 1985; Raven *et al* 1985).

8.24. cf Raven (1984, 1985, 1991).

8.25. The words "high-level" are intended to signal that the low-level measures of the kind produced by Walberg (1974) deflect attention away from the relevant issues.

8.26. Walberg (1985); Walberg and Haertel (1980); Moos (1979, 1980); Howard (1980, 1982, 1982, 1982)

8.27. It is of interest that, according to Kuhn (1962), Newton was unable to identify the practical implications of the theories he developed about how the universe worked: that came later.

8.28. Rogers (1962/1983)

9.1. See Janicke (1990) and Day and Klein (1987) for a wider demonstration of the failure of the political system to orchestrate communal action in the common good, and, in particular, of its inability to influence the TNCs. The reasons why market mechanisms could not be used to tackle the problems of the educational system are discussed in Raven (1989). The role of the market in producing rather than ameliorating these problems is discussed in Raven (1988) and will be discussed more fully in Raven (1993). See also Ekins (1986) and Robertson (1985).

9.2.   Toffler (1980)

9.3.   Schon (1972/73)

9.4.   Ferguson (1980)

9.5.   Raven (1989, 1992)

9.6.   Howard (1980, 1982, 1982, 1982)

9.7.   Howard (1980, 1982, 1982, 1982)

9.8.   But see Raven (1982) for the problems in evaluation of pilot programs and for a discussion of the stresses which participation in such experimentation cause.

9.9.   Rogers (1962, 1983); Roberts (1968, 1969); Schon (1972/73)

9.10.   Rogers (1962/1983); but see Raven (1985) for a discussion of the misunderstandings of these terms in education.

9.11.   What this indicates is a need to have a range of units studying and publicly debating "the same" topics and the need to have a range of personnel in education and the public service: to have some ideas men, some publicists, and some who work in the spaces between departments.

9.12.   It is worth noting that determination of the public interest is primarily a research based activity because it involves studying the long term personal and social consequences of different alternatives and the interactions between the effects of actions taken in different areas. However, the next stage will normally involve generating a range of options with demonstrably different consequences and making those options, together with information on their short and long-term consequences, available to the public so that the fact can emerge that there is not one public interest but a range of interests.

9.13.   Emery *et al* (1974)

9.14.   Day and Klein (1987)

10.1.   House (1991) has provided an excellent account of the need to get behind "data" to discern underlying and invisible structures and processes.

10.2.   An insightful and amusing account of the ways in which the universities stifle innovative research will be found in Nisbett (1990).

10.3.   Out of every 1000 AERA publications only 20 contain *new* data and in only 5 of those is the data substantive; the rest contain non-knowledge and are churned out to satisfy the 'publish or perish' machine which characterizes the entire output of research at the present time.

10.4.   Gardner (1990) has likewise emphasized the need to develop summative measures of school performance so that the public can be assured that they are getting value for money from educational programs without deflecting schools into low-level activities and also the need for tools to help teachers to administer high-level competency-oriented programs (although he does not, in fact, recognize the importance of more than a fraction of the competencies emphasized in this book).

10.5.   Salomon (1991) has provided excellent examples of the way in which intervention in one part of the system yields unexpected benefits and disbenefits elsewhere and also of the way in which interventions at one point are cancelled by reactions elsewhere in the system.

10.6.   Raven (1981)

10.7.   Levenstein (1975)

10.8.   McClelland (1982)

10.9.   Sigel (1985, 1986); Sigel and McGillicuddy (1984)

10.10.   For an excellent illustration of the non educational barriers to educational innovation see Schwartz in Searle (1985).

10.11.   Day and Klein (1987)

10.12.   These issues have been discussed at greater length in Raven (1991). The only way in which it is possible to throw light on the short and long-term, personal and societal, "intangible and hard-to-measure" consequences of changing processes is to adopt a variant of what Hamilton (1977) and his colleagues have termed "illuminative" evaluation. In this, personal observation, data collected through informal interviews, data obtained through the use of unobtrusive measures, and formal quantitative data are combined to yield an understanding of the processes involved. This in turn is used to generate an understanding of what the short and long-term outcomes of the process are likely to be. This process is heavily dependent on theory - but it is the only approach that has legitimacy in a situation in which there are no measures of the most important outcomes of the process (such as the effects on students' ability to undertake complex and demanding activities), in which the most important effects (such as economic and social development) will take many years to show up, and in which the most important barriers to the effective operation of the system are deep-seated, non-obvious, and systemic. The approach is in flat contradiction to that advocated by the *Joint Committee on Standards for the Evaluation of Educational Programs and Policies* (Stufflebeam et al 1981). It cuts across the qualitative/quantitative divide on which so much argument in the field of educational evaluation has focussed ([Jacob 1987, 1988; Atkinson et al 1988), but it has found unexpected endorsement in the work of House (1991) and Salomon (1991).

10.13.   The way in which the extraordinary requirements of effective evaluation can be approximated are hinted at in the previous footnote, and are discussed in more detail in Raven (1989, 1991). The problems which effective evaluation poses for evaluators and their deployment are discussed at greater length in several chapters in Searle (1985).

10.14.   Cherns (1970); Freeman (1973); Roberts (1968, 1969); Tizard (1990)

11.1.   Robinson (1983)

11.2.   The author and publisher are committed to producing another book which will spell out in greater detail what these are.

11.3.   I am indebted to Jack Whitehead for suggesting these questions.

REFERENCES

Adams, E. and Burgess, T. (1989). Teachers' Own Records. Windsor, England: NFER-Nelson.

Adams, E.A., Robbins, D. and Stephenson, J. (1981). Validity and Validation in Higher Education. Research Papers 1-4 and Summary Report. London: North East London Polytechnic, School of Independent Studies.

Aikin, W.M. (1942). The Story of the Eight Year Study. Adventure in American Education. Vol.I. New York: Harper Bros.

Atkinson, P., Delamont, S. and Hammersley, M. (1988). Qualitative research traditions: A British response to Jacob. Review of Educational Research, Vol.58, No.2, 231-250.

Bachman, J.G., Green, S. and Wirtanen, I.D. (1971). Youth in Transition III: Dropping Out - Problem or Symptom? Ann Arbor, Michigan: The Institute for Social Research.

Bachman, J.G., O'Malley, P.M. and Johnston, J. (1978). Adolescence to Adulthood: Change and Stability in the Lives of Young Men. Ann Arbor, Michigan: The Institute for Social Research.

Bandura, A. (1977). Social Learning Theory. Englewood Cliffs, New Jersey; Prentice-Hall.

Barnes, Emily A. and Young, Bess M. (1932). Unit of Work: Children and Architecture. Lincoln School, New York: Bureau of Publications, Teachers College, Columbia University for Lincoln School of Teachers College.

Barth, R.S. (1972). Open Education and the American School. New York: Agathon Press. Bellini, J. (1980). Rule Britannia: A Progress Report for Domesday 1986. London: Jonathan Cape.

Bennett, N. (1976). Teaching Styles and Pupil Progress. London: Open Books.

Berg, I. (1973). Education and Jobs: The Great Training Robbery. London: Penguin Books.

Bernstein, B. (1971). Class, Codes and Controls. London: Routledge and Kegan Paul.

Bernstein, B. (1975). Class and pedagogies: Visible and invisible. in W.B. Dockrell and D. Hamilton (Eds.), Rethinking Educational Research. London: Hodder and Stoughton.

Bestor, A. (1953). Educational Wastelands: The Retreat from Learning in our Public Schools. Urbana: University of Illinois Press.

Beuret, G. and Webb, A. (1983). Goals of Engineering Education. London: CNAA.

Bill, J.M., Trew, C.J. and Wilson, J.A. (1974). Early Leaving in Northern Ireland. Belfast: Northern Ireland Council for Educational Research.

Bouchard, T. and McGue, M. (1990). Genetic and rearing environmental influences on adult personality: An analysis of adopted twins reared apart. J. of Personality, March.

Bourne, R.S. (1916). The Gary Schools. New York: Houghton Mifflin.

Broadfoot, P. (1979). Assessment, Schools and Society. London: Methuen.

Bruner, J.S. (1965). Man: A Course of Study. Occasional Paper No. 3: Social Studies Curriculum Program. Cambridge, Massachusetts: Educational Services Inc.

Burgess, T. and Adams, E. (1986). Records for all at 16. in P. Broadfoot, (Ed.), Profiles and Records of Achievement. London: Holt, Rinehart and Winston.

Burgess, T. and Adams, E. (1986). Records of Achievement at 16. Windsor: NFER-Nelson

Burgess, T. and Pratt, J. (1970). Polytechnics in Pakistan. London: North East London Polytechnic.

Burns, A., Homel, R. and Goodnow, J. (1984). Conditions of life and parental values. Australian J. Psychology, 36, 219-237.

Caswell, H.L. (1942). Education in the Elementary School. New York: American Book Co.

Caswell, H.L. and Campbell, D.S. (1935). Curriculum Development. New York: American Book Co.

Centre for Educational Sociology, University of Edinburgh. (1977). Collaborative Research Dictionary.

Cherns, A.B. (1970). Relations between research institutions and users of research. International Social Science Journal, XXII, 226-42.

Chomsky, N. (1987). The Chomsky Reader. London: Serpent's Tail.

Collins, R. (1979). The Credential Society. New York: Academic Press.

Comber, L.C. and Keeves, J.P. (1973). Science Education in Nineteen Countries. Stockholm: Almquist and Wiksell: New York: John Wiley, The Halsted Press.

Counts, G.S. (1932/69). Dare the Schools Build a New Social Order? New York: John Day; (1969: Arno).

Cremin, L.A. (1961). The Transformation of the School. New York: Knopf.

Csikszentmihalyi, M. and LeFevre, J. (1989). Optimal experience in work and leisure. J. Pers. Soc. Psychol, 56, 815-822.

Curriculum Development Asssociates Inc. (1969/70). Man: A Course of Study. Washington, D.C.: Curriculum Development Asssociates Inc.

Day, P. and Klein, R. (1987). Accountabilities: Five Public Services. London: Tavistock Publications.

De Landsheere, V. (1977). On defining educational objectives. Evaluation in Education, 1, No.2, 73-190. Oxford: Pergamon Press.

Department of Education and Science (1989). National Curriculum: From Policy to Practice. London: HMSO.

Dewey, J. (1899). The School and Society. Chicago: University of Chicago Press.

Dewey, J. (1902). The Child and the Curriculum. Chicago: University of Chicago Press.

Dewey, J. (1910). How We Think. New York: D.C. Heath.

Dewey, J. (1916). Democracy and Education. New York: MacMillan.

Dockrell, B. (1991). The effects of system wide testing: Issues raised by a case study in a developing country. Studies in Educational Evaluation, Vol.17, 41-49.

Dore, R. (1976). The Diploma Disease. London: Allen and Unwin.

Dunn, W.R. and Hamilton D.D. (1985). The Determination of Priorities in the Postgraduate Education of Pharmacists. Unpublished Report: Glasgow University, Department of Education.

Education Policies Commission. (1938). The Purposes of Education in American Democracy. Washington, D.C.: National Education Assn.

Ekins, P. (1986). The Living Economy. London: Routledge.

Emery, F. et al. (1974). Futures We're In. Centre for Continuing Education, Australian National University.

Ferguson, M. (1980). The Aquarian Conspiracy: Personal and Social Transformation in the 1980s. London: Paladin.

Fivars, G and Gosnell, D. (1966). Nursing Evaluation: The Problem and the Process. Pittsburg Pennsylvania: Westinghouse Learning Corp.

Flanagan, J.C. (1976). Planning Life and Career Goals: A Cluster of Materials and Manuals. Monterey, California: CTB/ McGraw Hill.

Flanagan, J.C. (1978). Perspectives on Improving Education from a Study of 10,000 30-year-olds. New York: Praeger Publishers.

Flanagan, J.C. and Burns, R.K. (1955). The employee performance record. Harvard Business Review, 33, 95-102.

Flanagan, J.C. and Russ-Eft, D. (1975). An Empirical Study to Aid in Formulating Educational Goals. Palo Alto, California: American Institutes for Research.

Fores, M. and Pratt, J. (1980). Engineering: Our last chance. Higher Education Review, 12, 5-26.

Foshay, A.W. (1991). The curriculum matrix: Trancendence and mathematics. J. of Curriculum and Supervision, Vol.6, No.4, 277-293.

Fraley, A. (1981). Schooling and Innovation: The Rhetoric and the Reality. New York: Tyler Gibson.

Freedman, M. and Berg, I. (1978). Investment in education: Public policies and private risks. New Directions in Education and Work, 2, 19-34.

Freeman, F.C. (1973). A study of success and failure in industrial innovation. *in* B.R. Williams (Ed.), Science and Technology in Economic Growth. London: MacMillan.

Freire, P. (1970). Pedagogy of the Oppressed. London: Penguin Books.

French, W. et al. (1957). Behavioural Goals of General Education in High School. New York: Russell Sage Foundation.

Gallimore, R. (1985). The Accommodation of Instruction to Cultural Differences. Los Angeles: University of California, Dept. Psychiatry.

Galton, M. and Simon, B. (1980). Progress and Performance in the Primary Classroom. London: Routledge and Kegan Paul.

Galton, M., Simon, B. and Croll, P. (1980). Inside the Primary Classroom. London: Routledge and Kegan Paul.

Gardner, H. (1983). Frames of Mind: The Theory of Multiple Intelligences. New York: Basic Books.

Gardner, H. (1985). The Mind's New Science. New York: Basic Books.

Gardner, H. (1987). Developing the spectrum of human intelligence. Harvard Education Review, 57, 187-193.

Gardner, H. (1990). The difficulties of school: Probable causes, possible cures. *in* Literacy in America, DAEDALUS/Proceedings of the American Academy of Arts and Sciences, 119, 85-113.

Goodlad, J. (1983). A Place Called School. New York: McGraw Hill.

Goodlad, J., Klein, M.F. et al. (1974). Looking Behind the Classroom Door. Worthington, Ohio: Charles A. Jones Publishing Co.

Goodman, P. (1962). Compulsory Mis-Education. London: Penguin Books.

Gow, L. and McPherson, A. (Eds.). (1980). Tell Them From Me: Scottish School Leavers Write About School and Life Afterwards. Aberdeen University Press.

Graham, M.A., Raven, J. and Smith, P.C. (1987). Identification of high level competence: Cross-cultural analysis between British, American, Asian and Polynesian labourers. Unpublished MSS.

Grannis, J.C. (1983). Ecological observation of experimental education settings. Environment and Behaviour, 15, 21-52.

Gray, J. et al. (1983). Reconstructions of Secondary Education: Theory, Myth and Practice Since the War. London: Routledge and Kegan Paul.

Hamilton, D. (Ed.). (1977). Beyond the Numbers Game. London: MacMillan Education.

Hargreaves, A. (1988). The crisis of motivation and assessment. *in* A. Hargreaves and D. Reynolds (Eds.), Educational Policy: Controversies and Critiques. Lewes: Falmer Press.

Harlen, W. (1984). The impact of APU science work at LEA and school level. J. Curr. Studies, 16, 89-94.

Hatch, T.C. and Gardner, H. (1990). If Binet had looked beyond the classroom: The assessment of multiple intelligences. International Journal of Educational Research, 415-429.

Her Majesty's Government (1988). The Education Reform Bill. London: HMSO.

HMI. (Scotland) (1980). Learning and Teaching in Primary 4 and Primary 7. Edinburgh: HMSO.

HMI. (1990). A Survey of Balanced Science Courses in some Secondary Schools. London: Dept. Education and Science.

Hogan, R. (1990). Unmasking incompetent managers. Insight, May 21, 42-44.

Holt, J. (1977). Instead of Education. London: Penguin Books.

Hope, K. (1984). As Others See Us: Schooling and Social Mobility in Scotland and the United States. New York: Cambridge University Press.

House, E.R. (1991) Realism in Research. Educational Researcher, 20, 2-9.

Howard, E. (1980). Some Ideas on Improving School Climate. Denver: Colorado Department of Education.

Howard, E. (1982). Instrument to Assess the Educational Quality of Your School. Denver: Colorado Department of Education.

Howard, E. (1982). Involving students in school climate improvement. New Designs for Youth Development. Tucson, Arizona: Associations for Youth Development Inc.

Howard, E. (1982). Successful Practices for Making the Curriculum More Flexible. Denver: Colorado Department of Education.

Huff, S., Lake, D. and Schaalman, M.L. (1982). Principal Differences: Excellence in School Leadership and Management. Boston: McBer and Co.

Husen, T. and Postlethwaite, N. (Eds.). (1985). International Encyclopaedia of Education. London: Pergamon.

International Review of Applied Psychology. (1983). Special Issue dealing with the Relationship between Educational Institutions and Society, with Particular Reference to the Role of Assessment. Spring.

ITRU. (1979). The A-Z Study: Differences between improvers and non-improvers among young unskilled workers. Cambridge: The Industrial Training Research Unit.

Jackson, P.W (1986). The Practice of Teaching. New York: Teachers College Press.

Jacob, E. (1987). Qualitive research traditions: A review. Review of Educational Research, 57(1), 1-50.

Jacob, E. (1988). Clarifying qualitative research: A focus on traditions. Educational Researcher, 17(1), 16-24.

Janicke, Martin (1990). State Failure. Cambridge: Polity Press.

175

Jaques, E. (1976). A General Theory of Bureaucracy. London: Heinemann.

Jaques, E. (1989). Requisite Organization. Virginia: Cason Hall and Co.

Jencks, C., Smith, M., Acland, H., Bane, M.J., Cohen, D., Gintis, H., Heyns, B. and Michelson, S. (1972/3). Inequality: A Reassessment of the Effect of Family and Schooling in America. New York: Basic Books; London: England: Penguin Books.

Johnston, L.D. (1973). The American High School: Its Social System and Effects. Ann Arbor, Michigan: Institute for Social Research.

Johnston, L.D. and Bachman, J.G. (1976). Educational Institutions. in J.F. Adams (Ed.), Understanding Adolescence, IIIrd Edition. (290-315) Boston: Allyn and Bacon.

Kanter, R.M. (1985). The Change Masters: Corporate Entrepreneurs at Work. Hemel Hempstead: Unwin Paperbacks.

Kilpatrick, W.H. (1918). The project method. Teachers College Record, 19, 319-35.

Kilpatrick, W.H. (1926/1972). Foundations of Method. New York: MacMillan: (1972: Arno).

Kinsey, A.C. (1948). Sexual Behaviour in the Human Male. New York: Saunders.

Klemp, G.O., Huff, S.M. and Gentile, J.D.G. (1980). The Guardians of Campus Change: A Study of Leadership in Non Traditional College Programmes. Boston: McBer and Co.

Klemp, G.O. and McClelland, D.C. (1986). What characterises intelligent functioning among senior managers? in R.J. Sternberg and R.K. Wagner, Practical Intelligence. New York: Cambridge University Press.

Klemp, G.O., Munger, M.T. and Spencer, L.M. (1977). An Analysis of Leadership and Management Competencies of Commissioned and Non-Commissioned Naval Officers in the Pacific and Atlantic Fleets. Boston: McBer and Co.

Kohn, M.L. (1969). Class and Conformity: A Study in Values. Illinois: Dorsey Press.

Kohn, M.L. (1977). Class and Conformity: A Study in Values, Second Edition. Chicago Illinois: Chicago University Press.

Kuhn, T.S. (1962/1970). The Structure of Scientific Revolutions. Second, Enlarged Edition. Chicago: University of Chicago Press.

Levenstein. P. (1975). The Mother-Child Home Program. New York: Verbal Interaction Project.

Litton, F. and Raven, J. (1977/82). Aspects of Civics Education in Ireland, Final Report. Dublin: Institute of Public Administration. Also available in Collected Original Resources in Education, (1982), 6, (2), F4.E7.

Litwin, G.H. and Siebrecht, A. (1967). Integrators and entrepreneurs: Their motivation and effect on management. Hospital Progress, September.

176

MacBeath, J., Mearns, D., Thomson, B. and How, S. (1981). Social Education: The Scottish Approach. Glasgow: Jordanhill College of Education.

McClelland, D.C., Baldwin, A.L., Bronfenbrenner, U. and Strodtbeck, F.L. (1958). Talent and Society. Princeton, New Jersey: Van Nostrand.

McClelland, D.C. (1961). The Achieving Society. New York: Van Nostrand.

McClelland, D.C. (1962). On the psychodynamics of creative physical scientists. in H.E. Gruber (Ed.), Contemporary Approaches to Creative Thinking. New York: Atherton.

McClelland, D.C. (1964). The Roots of Consciousness. Princeton, New Jersey: Van Nostrand.

McClelland, D.C. (1965). Toward a theory of motive acquisition. American Psychologist, 20, 321-333.

McClelland, D.C. (1982). Education for Values. New York: Irvington Press.

McClelland, D.C. (1982). What behavioural scientists have learned about how children acquire values. in D.C. McClelland (Ed.), The Development of Social Maturity. New York: Irvington Press.

McClelland, D.C, Atkinson, J.W., Clark, R.A. and Lowell, E.L. (1958). A scoring manual for the achievement motive; Heynes, R.W., Veroff, J., and Atkinson, J.W. A scoring manual for the affiliation motive; Veroff, J. A scoring manual for the power motive. in J.W. Atkinson (Ed.), Motives in Fantasy, Action and Society. New York: Van Nostrand, chapters 12, 13, 14.

McClelland, D.C. and Burnham, D.H. (1976). Power is the great motivation. Harvard Business Review, 54, No.2.

McClelland, D.C. and Dailey, C. (1973). Evaluating New Methods of Measuring the Qualities Needed in Superior Foreign Service Workers. Boston: McBer and Co.

McClelland, D.C. and Dailey, C. (1974). Professional Competencies of Human Service Workers. Boston: McBer and Co.

McClelland, D.C. and Winter, D.G. (1969). Motivating Economic Achievement. New York: Free Press.

McGue, M. and Bouchard, T.J. (1989). Genetic and environmental determinants of information processing and special mental abilities: A twin analysis. in R.J. Sternberg (Ed.), Advances in the Psychology of Human Intelligence, Vol.5, (7-45). Hillsdale New Jersey: Lawrence Earlbaum.

MacKinnon, D.W. (1962). The nature and nurture of creative talent. American Psychologist, 17, 484-494.

Miller, K.A., Kohn, M.L. and Schooler, C. (1985). Educational self-direction and the cognitive functioning of students. Social Forces, 63, 923-944.

Miller, K.A., Kohn, M.L. and Schooler, C. (1986). Educational self-direction and personality. Amer. Sociol. Rev., 51, 372-390.

Mississippi State Dept. Education (1936). A Guide for Curriculum Planning. Jackson, Mississippi: State Dept. Education.

Moos, R.H. (1979). Educational climates. in H.J. Walberg, Educational Environments and Effects. Berkeley, California: McCutchan.

Moos, R.H. (1980). Evaluating classroom learning environments. Stud. Educ. Eval., 6, 239-252.

Morgan, G.A. (1986). Images of Organisation. Beverly Hills, California: Sage.

Morton-Williams, R., Finch, S. and Poll, C. (1966). Undergraduates Attitudes to School Teaching as a Career. London: Government Social Survey Department.

Morton-Williams, R., Finch, S., Poll, C., Raven, J., Ritchie, J. and Hobbs, E. (1968). Schools Council Enquiry One: Young School Leavers. London: HMSO.

Morton-Williams, R., Raven, J. and Ritchie, J. (1971). Sixth Form Teachers and Pupils. London: Schools Council/Books for Schools.

MSC (1984). TVEI Review, 1984. London: MSC.

National Society for the Study of Education. (1926). Twenty Sixth Year Book: The Foundation and Techniques of Curriculum Making. Bloomfield, Illinois: Public School Publishing Co.

Newton Public Schools. (1972). Blowing on a Candle. Newton, Massachusetts: Public Schools.

Nisbett, R.E. (1990). The Anti-creativity Letters: Advice from a Senior Tempter to a Junior Tempter. American Psychologist, 45, 1078-1082.

Nuffield Science Team. (1967). Biology: Teachers Guides Vols. I-V and Texts I-V. London: Longmans/Penguin.

Nuttgens, P. (1988). What Should We Teach and How Should We Teach It? Aldershot: Wildwood House.

ORACLE. See Galton & Simon (1980); Galton, Simon & Croll (1980); Simon & Willcocks (1981).

Parker, F.W. (1894, 1969). Talks on Pedagogics. New York: Arno Press (originally, E.L.Kellogg).

Payne, G., Ford, G. and Ulas, M. (1979). Education and Social Mobility: Some Social and Theoretical Developments. Organisation of Sociologists in Polytechnics. Paper No.8.

Pellegrini, A.D., Brody, G.H. and Sigel, I.E. (1985). Parents book-reading habits with their children. J. Ed. Psychol., 77, 332-340.

Popkewitz, T.S. et al. (1982). The Myth of Educational Reform. Wisconsin: University Press.

Price, P.B., Taylor, C.W., Nelson, D.E. et al. (1971). Measurement and Predictors of Physician Performance: Two Decades of Intermittently

Sustained Research. Salt Lake City: University of Utah, Dept. of Psychology.

Purves, A.C. (1973). Literature Education in Ten Countries. Stockholm: IEA; New York: John Wiley, The Halsted Press.

Rathbone, C.H. (Ed.). (1971). Open Education: The Informal Classroom. New York: Citation Press.

Raven, J. (1973). The attainment of non-academic objectives in education. International Review of Education, 19, 305-344.

Raven, J. (1976). Pupil Motivation and Values. Dublin: Irish Association for Curriculum Development.

Raven, J. (1977). Education, Values and Society: The Objectives of Education and the Nature and Development of Competence. Oxford, England: Oxford Psychologists Press.

Raven, J. (1980). Parents, Teachers and Children: An Evaluation of an Educational Home Visiting Programme. Edinburgh: The Scottish Council for Research in Education. Distributed in North America by the Ontario Institute for Studies in Education, Toronto.

Raven, J. (1981). Early intervention: A selective review of the literature. Collected Original Resources in Education, 5, F1C6.

Raven, J. (1982). What's in a name? Some problems in the evaluation of pilot projects. Scottish Educational Review, 14, 15-22.

Raven, J. (1984). Competence in Modern Society: Its Identification, Development and Release. Oxford, England: Oxford Psychologists Press.

Raven, J. (1984). Some limitations of the standards. Evaluation and Program Planning, 7, 363-370.

Raven, J. (1985). The institutional framework required for, and process of, educational evaluation: Some lessons from three case studies. in B. Searle (Ed.), Evaluation in World Bank Education Projects: Lessons from Three Case Studies. Washington, D.C.: The World Bank, Education and Training Dept. Report EDT5 141-170.

Raven, J. (1986). A nation really at risk: A review of Goodlad's "A Place Called School". Higher Education Review, 18, 65-79.

Raven, J. (1987). Deficiencies in Current Practice in Teacher Education and their Implications for the Role of Psychologists in Teacher Education. Paper presented to the BPS Education Section Conference, October 1987.

Raven, J. (1987). Learning to Teach in Primary Schools: Some Reflections. Collected Original Resources in Education, 11, F3,D07.

Raven, J. (1987). Values, diversity and cognitive development. Teachers College Record, 89, 21-38.

Raven, J. (1988). The assessment of competencies. *in* H.D. Black and W.B. Dockrell (Eds.), New Developments in Educational Assessment: British Journal of Educational Psychology, Monograph Series No.3, 98-126.

Raven, J. (1988). Choice in a modern economy: New concepts of democracy and bureaucracy. *in* S. Maital (Ed.), Applied Behavioural Economics, Vol II. (812-824) Brighton, England: Wheatsheaf.

Raven, J. (1988). Developing the talents and competencies of all our children. Gifted International, 5, 8-40.

Raven, J. (1988). A model of competence, motivation and its assessment. *in* H. Berlak (Ed.), Assessing Academic Achievement: Issues and Problems. Madison, Wisconsin: National Center for Effective Secondary Schools.

Raven, J. (1988). School based evaluation and professional research. Studies in Educational Evaluation, 14, 176-191.

Raven, J. (1989). Democracy, bureaucracy and the psychologist. The Psychologist, Vol.2, No.11, November, 458-466.

Raven, J. (1989). Equity in diversity: The problems posed by values - and their resolution. *in* F. Macleod (Ed.), Families and Schools: Issues in Accountability and Parent Power. (59-101) Brighton, England: Falmer Press.

Raven, J. (1989). Giving information teeth. Unpublished mss.

Raven, J. (1989). Parents, education and schooling. *in* C. Desforges (Ed.), British Journal of Educational Psychology, Monograph Series No.4, Special Issue on Early Childhood Education, 47-67.

Raven, J. (1990). The Management of Innovation in Modern Society. Submitted to Human Relations.

Raven, J. (1991). The Tragic Illusion: Educational Testing. Some Problems with Conventional Testing - And a Way Forward. New York: Trillium Press; Oxford, England: Oxford Psychologists Press.

Raven, J. (1992). Equity in Diversity. New York: Trillium Press.

Raven, J. (1993). The New Wealth of Nations: A New Enquiry into the Nature and Origins of the Wealth of Nations . New York: Trillium Press; Oxford, England: Oxford Psychologists Press.

Raven, J. and Dolphin, T. (1978). The Consequences of Behaving: The Ability of Irish Organisations to Tap Know-How, Initiative, Leadership and Goodwill. Edinburgh: The Competency Motivation Project.

Raven, J., Hannon, B., Handy, R., Benson, C. and Henry, E.A. (1975). A Survey of Attitudes of Post Primary Teachers and Pupils, Volume 1: Teachers' Perceptions of Educational Objectives and Examinations. Dublin: Irish Association for Curriculum Development.

Raven, J., Hannon, B., Handy, R., Benson, C. and Henry, E.A. (1975). A Survey of Attitudes of Post Primary Teachers and Pupils, Volume 2: Pupils' Perceptions of Educational Objectives and their Reactions to

School and School Subjects. Dublin: Irish Association for Curriculum Development.

Raven, J., Johnstone, J. and Varley, T. (1985). Opening the Primary Classroom. Edinburgh: The Scottish Council for Research in Education.

Raven, J. and Litton, F. (1976). Irish pupils' civic attitudes in an international context. Oideas, Spring, 16-30.

Raven, J. and Varley, T. (1984). Some classrooms and their effects: A study of the feasibility of measuring some of the broader outcomes of education. Collected Original Resources in Education, 8, No.1, F4 G6.

Raven, J. and Whelan, C.T. (1976). Irish adults' perceptions of their civic institutions. in J. Raven, C.T. Whelan, P.A. Pfretzschner and D.M. Borock, Political Culture in Ireland. Dublin: Institute of Public Administration.

Ravitch, D. (1974). The Great Schools Wars. New York: Basic Books.

Ravitch, D. (1983). The Troubled Crusade. New York: Basic Books.

Reimer, E. (1971). School is Dead. London: Penguin Books.

Ritchie, J. and Morton-Williams, R. (1971). Sixth Form Enquiry, Phase IIB: Sixth Form Leavers. London: Schools Council Publications.

Roberts, E.B. (1968). A basic study of innovators: How to keep and capitalize on their talents. Research Management, XI, 249-266.

Roberts, E.B. (1969). Entrepreneurship and technology. in W.H. Gruber and D.G. Marquis (Eds.), The Human Factor in the Transfer of Technology. Cambridge, Massachusetts: MIT Press.

Robertson, J. (1985). Future Work: Jobs, Self-Employment and Leisure After the Industrial Age. Aldershot: Gower/Maurice Temple Smith.

Robinson, D.W. (1983). Patriotism and Economic Control: the Censure of Harold Rugg. Rutgers University, New Jersey: D.Ed. Dissertation. 1984: Ann Arbor, Michigan: University Microfilms International.

Robinson, J.P. et al. (1969). Job satisfaction researches. Personnel and Guidance Journal, 45, 371-379.

Robinson, J.P. et al. (1969). Measures of Occupational Attitudes and Occupational Characteristics. Ann Arbor: University of Michigan, Survey Research Center.

Rogers, E.M. (1962/1983). Diffusions of Innovations. New York: Free Press.

Rugg, H. (1926). in NSSE Year Book 1926. Rugg, H. and Shumaker, A. (1928). The Child-Centered School. Yonkers: George Harrap.

Salomon, G. (1991). Transcending the Qualitative-Quantitative Debate: The Analytic and Systemic Approaches to Educational Research. Educational Researcher, 20, 11-18.

Schlichter, C. (1986). Talents unlimited: Applying the multiple talent approach in mainstream and gifted programs. in J.S. Renzulli, Systems and Models for Developing Programs for the Gifted and Talented. Connecticut: Creative Learning Press.

Schneider, C., Klemp, G.O. and Kastendiek, S. (1981). The Balancing Act: Competencies of Effective Teachers and Mentors in Degree Programs for Adults. Boston: McBer and Co.

Schon, D. (1971/73). Beyond the Stable State. London: Penguin.

Schon, D. (1987). Educating the Reflective Practitioner. San Francisco: Jossey-Bass.

Schools Council Humanities Curriculum Project. (1970-72). 1,235 packages of materials. Published by Heinemann Education Books, London.

Schools Council Integrated Science Project. (1970-72). Patterns: Teachers' Guides 1 & 2; Pupils' Manuals: 1 & 2. London: Schools Council Publications Co.

Schwartz, H.H. (1987). Perceptions, judgment and motivation in manufacturing entrepreneurs. J. Econ. Behavior and Organisation, 8, 543-566.

Searle, B. (Ed.). (1985). Evaluation in World Bank Education Projects; Lessons from Three Case Studies. Washington D.C.: The World Bank, Education and Training Dept, Report No.EDT5.

Sharpe, P. (1972). Sixth Form Enquiry, Phase II. Full-time A-Level Students at Colleges of Further Education. London: Schools Council Publications Co.

Sigel, I.E. (Ed.). (1985). Parent Belief Systems: The Psychological Consequences for Children. Hillside, New Jersey: Earlbaum.

Sigel, I.E. (1986). Reflections on the belief-behavior connection: Lessons learned from a research program on parental belief systems and teaching strategies. in R.D. Ashmore and D.M. Brodzinsky (Eds.), Thinking about the Family: Views of Parents and Children. Hillsdale, New Jersey: Earlbaum.

Sigel, I.E. and McGillicuddy-DeLisi, A.V. (1984). Parents as teachers of their children: A distancing behavior model. in A.D. Pellegrini and T.D. Yawkey (Eds.), The Development of Oral and Written Language in Social Contexts. Norwood, New Jersey: Ablex.

Simon, B. and Willcocks, J. (Eds.). (1981). Research and Practice in the Primary Classroom. London: Routledge and Kegan Paul.

"Sneddon" Report (1978). Learning to Teach. Edinburgh: Scottish Education Department: HMSO.

Spearman, C. (1927). The Nature of "Intelligence" and the Principles of Cognition. Second Edition. London: MacMillan.

Stassen, H.H., Lykken, D.T. and Bomben, G. (1988). The within-pair similarity of twins reared apart. Eur. Arch. Psychaotr. Neurol. Sci., 237, 244-252.

Sternberg, R.J. (1986). Intelligence Applied. New York: Harcourt, Brace, Jovanovitch.

Stratemeyer, F.B., Forkner, H.L., McKim, M.C. and Passow A.H. (1947). Developing a Curriculum for Modern Living. New York: Teachers College; Columbia University Press.

Stufflebeam Joint Committee on Standards for Educational Evaluation. (1981). Standards for Evaluations of Educational Programs, Projects and Materials. New York: McGraw Hill.

Sykes, A.J.M. (1969). Navvies: Their work attitudes. Sociology, 3, 21f and 157f.

Taylor, C.W. (1971). All Our Students Are Educationally Deprived. Salt Lake City, Utah: University of Utah Press.

Taylor, C.W. (1974). Multiple talent teaching. Today's Education, March/April, 71-74.

Taylor, C.W. (1976). All our Children are Educationally Deprived. Salt Lake City, Utah: University of Utah Press.

Taylor, C.W. (1985). Cultivating multiple creative talents in students. Journal for the Educationally Gifted, Vol.VIII, No.3, 187-198.

Taylor, C.W. (1986). Cultivating simultaneous student growth in both multiple creative talents and knowledge. in J.S. Renzulli, Systems and Models for Developing Programs for the Gifted and Talented. Connecticut: Creative Learning Press.

Taylor, C.W. and Barron, F. (Eds.). (1963). Scientific Creativity. New York: Wiley.

Taylor, C.W., Smith, W.R. and Ghiselin, B. (1963). The creative and other contributions of one sample of research scientists. in C.W. Taylor and F. Barron (Eds.), Scientific Creativity: Its Recognition and Development. New York: Wiley.

Tellegen, A., Lykken, D.T., Bouchard, T.J., Wilcox, K.J., Segal, N.L. and Rich, S. (1988). Personality similarity in twins reared apart and together. J. of Personality and Social Psychology, Vol.54, No.6, 1031-1039.

Thorndike, R.L. (1973). Reading Comprehension in Fifteen Countries. Stockholm: Almquist and Wiksell; New York: John Wiley, The Halsted Press.

Thurow, L.C. (1983). Dangerous Currents: The State of Economics. New York: Random House.

Tippett, J.S. et al. (1927). Curriculum Making in an Elementary School. New York: Teachers College Press.

Tizard, B. (1990). Research and policy: Is there a link? The Psychologist, 3, 435-440.

Toffler, A. (1980). The Third Wave. New York: Bantam Books.

Tomlinson, T.M. and Tenhouten, D. (1976). Awareness, Achievement Strategies and Ascribed Status of Elites. Washington, D.C.: National Institute of Education. Unpublished Report.

Torney, J.V., Oppenheim, A.N. and Farnen, R. (1975). Civic Education in Ten Countries. New York: John Wiley, The Halsted Press.

Travers, R.M.W. (Ed.). (1973). Second Handbook of Research on Teaching. Chicago: Rand McNally.

Tyler, R.W. (1936). Defining and measuring the objectives of progressive education. Educational Research Bulletin, XV, 67f.

Van Beinum, H. (1965). The Morale of the Dublin Busman. London: Tavistock Institute of Human Relations.

Walberg, H.J. (Ed.). (1974). Evaluating Educational Performance. A Sourcebook of Methods. Berkeley, California: McCutchan.

Walberg, H.J. (1985). Classroom psychological environment. in T. Husen and N. Postlethwaite, International Encyclopaedia of Education. London: Pergamon.

Walberg, H.J. and Haertel, D. (1980). Validity and use of educational environmental assessments. Studies in Educational Evaluation, 6, 225-238.

Waller, N.G., Kojetin, B.A., Bouchard, T.J., Lykken, D.T. and Tellegen, A. (1989). Genetic and environmental influences on religious interests, attitudes and values: A study of twins reared apart and together. To be published in Psychological Science.

Walters, J. and Garner, H. (1986). The crystallizing experience. in R. Steinberg, (Ed.), Conceptions of Giftedness. New York: Cambridge University Press.

Whiting, D. (Ed.). (1972). Blowing on a Candle: the Flavour of Change. Newton, Massachusetts: Newton Public Schools.

Willis, P. (1977). Learning to Labour. Farnborough: Saxon House.

Winter, D.G. (1979). An Introduction to Leadership and Management Education and Training: Theory and Research. Boston: McBer and Co.

Winter, D.G. and McClelland, D.C. (1963). The classic personal style. J. Abn. Soc. Psychol., 67, 254-265.

Winter, D.G., McClelland, D.C. and Stewart, A.J. (1981). A New Case for the Liberal Arts. San Francisco: Jossey Bass.

Wittrock, M.C. (Ed.). AERA. (1986). Handbook of Research on Teaching: Third Edition. New York: AERA.

Wright, G.S. (1950). Core Curriculum in Public High Schools: An Enquiry into Practices, 1949. Office of Education Bulletin No.5. Washington, D.C.; Federal Security Agency.

Wright, G.S. (1958). Block-Time Classes and the Core Program in the Junior High School. Bulletin 1958, No.6. US Dept. Health, Education and Welfare. Washington, D.C.: US Government Printing Office.

Young, M.F.D. (1971). (Ed.). Knowledge and Control. New Directions for the Sociology of Education. London: Collier-Macmillan.